Jan 1972

Feb. 25
4:30

THE FABULATORS

THE FABULATORS

ROBERT SCHOLES

NEW YORK OXFORD UNIVERSITY PRESS 1967

025818

IN MEMORIAM
    L.F.B.
        FABULATOR VIRGINIBUS PUERISQUE

This Inclination to Fables, which is common to all Men, is not the effect of Reasoning, nor does it arise from Imitation, or Custom; it is natural to them, and is rivetted in the very Frame and Disposition of the Soul.

(from Bishop Huet's letter
on the origin of fiction,
the English translation of 1720)

ACKNOWLEDGMENTS

A number of people and institutions have contributed in various ways to the making of this book. I am grateful to them all. Walter Rideout and the late John Enck of the University of Wisconsin first directed my attention to some of the fabulators through Wisconsin's excellent series of readings by contemporary novelists in 1963–64. John Enck's interviews with these writers, published in *Wisconsin Studies in Contemporary Literature,* have provided me with much valuable food for thought. I am grateful also to the current editor of that excellent periodical, L. S. Dembo, for permission to quote from two of those interviews.

Mr. Francis Brown of the *New York Times Book Review* quickened my interest in John Barth by asking me to write a piece on his earlier work and to review *Giles Goat-Boy.* For this I thank him and I also thank the many later reviewers who disagreed with me and stimulated my thinking. Miss Charlotte Kohler, editor of the *Virginia*

Quarterly Review, and Louis Rubin, editor of the *Hollins Critic*, first published my work on Durrell and Vonnegut. I am grateful to them for that and for permission to include much of this material in Chapters 2 and 3 of this book.

My own academic home—the School of Letters at the University of Iowa—has done much to facilitate my work. For this I am grateful to Director John Gerber and President Howard Bowen.

For practical criticism of my manuscript I am happy to thank my old friend and colleague Carl Klaus—a master of rhetoric—and my editor Whitney Blake. Their pointed criticisms helped me to strengthen a number of sections of the book. And Mrs. Patricia Benton of the Oxford University Press provided indispensable editorial amenities.

For stimulating discussion I am grateful to many students, colleagues, and friends—among whom I must single out Phillip Cummins of the Philosophy Department at the University of Iowa, whose thoughts on *Giles Goat-Boy* helped me formulate my own; Lawrence Lipking of Princeton, whose cryptic comment on my study of Vonnegut make me think a bit harder; and the Great Birdo—adept of Baum and Barth—who told me more than she knew.

At the British Museum, the Superintendent of the North Reading Room was especially kind, disturbing a display of early printing to allow me access to Caxton's *Fables*, with the first English version of the tale of King and fabulator. The illustration on p. 9 was reproduced from this copy with permission of the British Museum.

June 1967   R.S.

CONTENTS

CHAPTER 1
PRELIMINARIES

I OF CRITICS AND CRITICISM

We should always be suspicious of criticism, and especially now. Because the mere production of it, apart from its quality, may do a man good in an academic career, much of it is produced with its author's eye on the wrong object. Thus we should always be ready to ask whether we need it and how we can use it. And we should remember that even the critic who has his eye on the right object—his subject matter—must by definition be an arrogant fellow to ask us to read him. He must assume he knows something we do not, either because he is more learned, more thoughtful, more sensitive, or just plain smarter than we are.

The book-reviewer justifies his existence by reading books we haven't read and offering us his opinion of them—for whatever it is worth. The critic, on the other hand, presumes to tell us how to read a book we may have read already. There are critics, of course, who tell us not how to

3

interpret but how to judge literary works. But this judicial or evaluative criticism is not directed at the literary work itself so much as at the work's audience. A critic who evaluates must begin with his personal "I like it" or "I don't like it." From that point, in discussing what is right or wrong with the work under consideration, he is saying to his audience, "Be like me. Make yourself as much like me as you can, and you will judge accurately in this matter. You will develop taste, for to have taste is to be like me." He may choose to call himself "high-cult" and try by scorn to drive the culture and the brows of his audience to his own lofty elevation. But whatever his method, if he tries to persuade you to accept *his* judgment, he must persuade you to see things his way. And the only justification for this is that his way is better than yours—even for you. This incredibly presumptuous process is known as education. A teacher really teaches not his subject but his view of his subject. When his students are as much like him as they can be, it is time for them to try another teacher and another view; until they become so inflexible as to be beyond instruction. Then they are ready to teach others.

I paint this situation in its darkest colors—but with as much fidelity as irony—in order to forewarn and forearm my readers. As George tells Martha before the last round of *Who's Afraid of Virginia Woolf?*, I want you on your feet and fighting, gentle reader, before I get serious. I do presume to educate you. I make one or more of the arrogant assumptions that teacher or critic must make about his relationship with an audience. I think I have things to tell you that you do not know. I think I can show you things in the works I discuss that you might not otherwise see. I think I can make more available to you the manifold pleasures that the writers I call fabulators have given me. I will trade my eyes for your ears.

The circumstances of such an intimate transaction make it only fair that I say something about myself. A mere *caveat emptor* is not enough. I must tell you something of the biases that warp my woof. The critic, who preserves many fancies, likes usually to pretend his work comes from some highly impersonal criticism gland, which would perform more or less identically if it happened to be secreted (and secreting) in some other human habitation. I want to begin by denying any pretense to impersonality on behalf of this work. It is the work of a particular man, who likes certain things because he is the sort of man to whom certain things appeal.

My love for fabulation has its roots in the reading I first learned to like. The reading I liked best as a boy was the most imaginative I could find. In my childhood, Mt. Olympus, The Emerald City, and the great world tree Ygdrasil were parts of the same, continuous geography. Older, I turned to historical novels and detective fiction. I remember vividly an interview at the Dartmouth Club in New York, during which I innocently made my reading practices known. I was not admitted to Dartmouth. At Yale I scandalized my first real English teacher by preferring Spenser to Chaucer. And though I have learned to know Chaucer's considerable virtues and admire them, I cannot—and would not—reverse my earlier opinion. From then until now I have been reading, finding writers like Conrad and Faulkner to revere and others like Joyce and Proust to admire. But it seems to me now that all these years I have been waiting for something, waiting for my own kind of writer to come along. Now, I recognize in the writers I have called fabulators the proper grown-up fare for such a boy as I was. And I am most grateful. This book, then, is written partly just to express my own joy of discovery. These artists, mostly Americans of my own generation— that used to be called silent—are wonderful writers, true fabulators, who have made reading once again for me a magical experience.

II   OF FABULATORS AND FABULATION

This lovely word, "fabulator," dropped out of our language a few years ago—just in time for me to pick it up and reintroduce it here. It is of course a gimmick, an attention-getter. But I think it is also an honest attempt to find a word for something that needs one; to find a word, moreover, that needs only a little tinkering to adapt it to its new function. As it happened (as it was meant to happen, we Bokononists would say), I came across the word just as I was beginning this project, and it helped to illuminate for me the nature of my subject. I found the word in the eighth fable of Alfonce, as these fables were Englished by Caxton in 1484 for one of the first books printed in Britain. Like all good fables it is instructive in many things beyond its immediate moral. No dictionary can teach us as much about fabulators and fabulation as this little tale. Which is quite as it should be.

❡ The eyght fable is of the difcyple / and of
the fheep /

Difcyple was fomtyme / whiche
toke his playfyre to reherce and
telle many fables / the whiche
prayd to his mayfter / that he
wold reherce vnto hym a long
fable / To whome the mayfter anfuerd / kepe and
beware wel that hit happe not to vs / as it happed
to a kyng and to his fabulatour And the difcyple
anfuerd / My mayfter I pray the to telle to me
how it befelle / And thenne the mayfter fayd to
his defcyple / ❡ Somtyme was a kynge whiche
hadde a fabulatour / the whiche reherced to
hym at euery tyme / that he wold fleep fyue
fables for to reioyffhe the kynge / and for to
make hym falle in to a flepe / It befelle thenne
on a daye / that the kynge was moche forowful
and fo heuy / that he coude in no wyfe falle a
flepe / And after that the fayd fabulatour had
told and reherced his fyue fables / the kynge
defyred to here more / And thenne the fayd
fabulatour recyted vnto hym thre fables wel
fhorte / And the kynge thenne fayd to hym / I
wold fayne here one wel longe / And thenne
fhalle I leue wel the flepe / The fabulatour
thenne reherced vnto hym fuche a fable / Of a
ryche man whiche wente to the market or feyre
for to bye fheep / the which man bought a
thowfand fheep / And as he was retornynge fro
the feyre / he cam vnto a Ryuer / and by caufe
of the grete waiues of the water he coude not
paffe ouer the brydge / Neuertheles he wente
foo longe to and fro on the Ryuage of the fayd

Ryuer / that at the laft he fonde a narowe way /
vpon the whiche myght paffe fcant ynough thre
fheep attones / And thus he paffed and had them
ouer one after another / And hyderto reherced
of this fable / the fabulatour felle on flepe / And
anon after the kynge awoke the fabulatour / and
fayd to hym in this manere / I pray the that
thow wylt make an ende of thy fable / And the
fabulatour anfuerd to hym in this manere   Syre
this Ryuer is ryght grete / and the fhip is lytyl /
wherfore late the marzhaunt doo pafs ouer his
fheep / And after I fhalle make an ende of my
fable / And thenne was the kynge wel appeafed
and pacyfyed / ⁋ And therfore be thow content
of that I haue reherced vnto the / For there is
folke fuperftycious or capaxe / that they may not
be contented with fewe wordes

From the very construction of this fable we can learn
something. It is in the form of a tale (about the sheep)
within a tale (about king and fabulator) within a tale
(about master and disciple). The enclosing or frame tale
of master and disciple is not brought completely to an end,
but we are led to assume that the tale of king and fabulator
must have satisfied the disciple and effectively silenced his
request for a long fable. The next tale, of king and fabulator, is neatly rounded off, with the king "well appeased
and pacified." The innermost tale, which we might call a
shaggy sheep story, is by its nature unending. Though en-
closed by the others it is not shut off but allowed to continue in our imaginations toward an "after" that is as
vaguely located in the future as the "sometime" which
begins the two outer tales is located in the past. This struc-

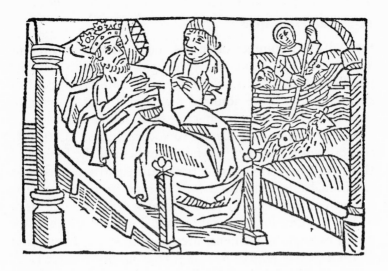

¶ The eyght fable is of the difcyple / And of the fkeep /

A Difcyple was fomtyme / whiche toke his playfyr to relerce and telle many fables / the whiche prayd to his mayfter / that he wold relerce vnto hym a long fable / To whome the mayfter anfuerd / kepe and beware wel that hit happe not to vs / as it happed to a kyng and to his fabulatour And the difcyple anfuerd / My mayfter I pray the to telle to me how it befelle / And thenne the mayfter fayd to his difcyple ¶ Somtyme was a kynge whiche hadde a fabulatour / the whiche relerced to hym at euery tyme / that he wold fleep fyue fables for to reioyffhe the kynge / and for to make hym falle in to a fleep / It bifelle thenne on a daye / that the kynge was moche forowful and fo heuy / that he coude in no wyfe falle a fleep / And after that the fayd fabulatour hadr told and relerced

The King and his Fabulator: from the eighth fable of Alfonce, published by Caxton in 1484. (*British Museum*)

ture tells us a number of things about fabulation. First of all, it reveals an extraordinary delight in design. With its wheels within wheels, rhythms and counterpoints, this shape is partly to be admired for its own sake. A sense of pleasure in form is one characteristic of fabulation.

The structure also, by its very shapeliness, asserts the authority of the shaper, the fabulator behind the fable. (In this case it is Caxton, partly translating, partly reworking a traditional tale introduced into Europe from the East by a Christianized Spanish Jew, who changed his name from Moses to Peter in 1106 and compiled a book of fables for use as exempla in sermons, including this one, *Exemplum XII: De rege et fabulatore suo.*) The authority of the fabulator over his fable is not only asserted by the ingenuity of the fabulation, however; this authority is reinforced by the relations among the characters in the two outer tales. As master is to disciple, so is fabulator to king. The king desperately needs this artist of the story to "rejoice" him and to enable him to relax—especially when the king is "sorrowful" and "heavy." The fabulator is important to the extent that he can rejoice and refresh us. And his ability to produce joy and peace depends on the skill with which he fabulates. Delight in design, and its concurrent emphasis on the art of the designer, will serve in part to distinguish the art of the fabulator from the work of the novelist or the satirist. Of all narrative forms, fabulation puts the highest premium on art and joy.

In using the word "fabulator" to designate certain modern writers of fiction, I mean to emphasize these qualities of art and joy, of course. I also hope to make the word suggest other, related qualities. Fables traditionally have lent themselves to preaching, either as exempla in medieval sermons or directly through moral tags appended to the tales themselves—or both. This didactic quality seems to me also characteristic of modern fabulation—but in ways which will need considerable qualification as we consider specific authors and instances. For the moment, suffice it to say that modern fabulation, like the ancient fabling of Aesop, tends away from the representation of reality but returns toward actual human life by way of ethically controlled fantasy. Many fabulators are allegorists. But the modern fabulators allegorize in peculiarly modern ways.

III   THE MODERN FABULATORS

It seems to me that the emergence of fabulation in recent fiction is not only an exciting development in itself; it also provides one answer to the great question of where fiction could go after the realistic novel. There are other answers, of course. The cinema provides a particularly frightening one for those of us who love words, because it threatens to take over from the word-smiths the business of story-telling. There are many aspects of this relation of cinema to fiction. I wish to touch on just one of them here before returning to the relationship between fabulation and novel-writing. And that one is the way that cinema gives the *coup de grâce* to a dying realism in written fiction. Realism purports —has always purported—to subordinate the words themselves to their referents, the things the words point to. Realism exalts Life and diminishes Art, exalts things and diminishes words. But when it comes to representing *things*, one picture *is* worth a thousand words, and one motion picture is worth a million. In the face of competition from cinema, fiction must abandon its attempt to "represent reality" and rely more on the power of words to stimulate the imagination. A picture must have a frame or an edge, but a word has no limit to its reverberations. Nature can never be merely recorded in words, for words are human creations and they inevitably lend their referents a human meaning and human value. They can never be neutral.

The growing awareness of this aspect of language has led some writers of fiction—notably the French "new" novelist Alain Robbe-Grillet—to resist it and "dehumanize" their writing. Robbe-Grillet has attempted this mainly by eliminating his metaphors, which he sees as the most pervasive and insidious way that language insists on humanizing everything that it represents. But this cannot solve the problem, because all language is a human product and thus must humanize all it touches. The writer must either acknowledge this and accept it as one of the terms of his work or turn to a wordless art like cinema—as M. Robbe-Grillet has so brilliantly done on occasion. For the writer who is willing to accept the word as his medium, however, other problems exist. He must move away from the pseudo-objectivity of realism toward a romance or an irony which will exploit language's distinctively human perspective on life. In competition with the cold and lidless eye of cinema the sightless book must turn to the dark world of the imagination, illuminating it by the uniquely human vision to be found in words.

Fabulation, then, means a return to a more verbal kind of fiction. It also means a return to a more fictional kind. By this I mean a less realistic and more artistic kind of narrative: more shapely, more evocative; more concerned with ideas and ideals, less concerned with things. I am not proposing here an airy program for the future of fiction. I

am talking about what is going on all around us. The fabulators are here and working. In England William Golding,
Iris Murdoch, and Lawrence Durrell are clearly committed
to this mode of fiction. Anthony Burgess has moved this
way, and in his last work even Kingsley Amis tried fabulation. In America Nabokov and a host of younger men can
properly be called fabulators. There are, in fact, too many
to deal with in a single book. In the pages that follow, I
have singled out only a few for individual treatment: Lawrence Durrell and Iris Murdoch from English fiction; Kurt
Vonnegut, Jr., Terry Southern, John Hawkes, and John
Barth from American. It is not my intention to plod through
every work of each of these writers, nor do I think that I
shall be dealing with all of the current fabulators of interest and achievement. Far from it. But I think the writers
I have chosen to discuss illustrate the range and vigor of
modern fabulation. Their work varies in value, I believe,
from the interesting to the great, but I shall not be concerned mainly with evaluation. My aim is really quite simple. I wish to broaden the audience for these writers a bit,
and perhaps deepen it as well. The reactions to their work
which I have found both in reading reviews and talking to
people seem to me quite confused, often baffled. Even
those who express their liking for this kind of writing are
often hesitant and embarrassed about it. Both the hospita-
ble and the inhospitable, both the plain readers and the
fancy reviewers, have trouble in adjusting to these works.
Much of the trouble comes from inadequate understanding
of this new literary mode I have called fabulation. The
trouble is aggravated by the absence of terminology in
which to discuss it. Evaluation and appreciation depend
helplessly on recognition of kind, and recognition requires

appropriate linguistic categories. As long as we expect a nectarine to taste like either a peach or a plum we are bound to be disappointed. But once we assimilate this new category—nectarine—we begin to know what we are dealing with and how to react to it. We can judge and appreciate.

My intention in introducing the term "fabulation" is to provide a new name for these new literary artifacts. Once we can see them not as misfits which have failed to become proper novels or satires or whatever, we can begin to see them as themselves. Fabulation, finally, can mean not what I say but what these works are. When that is accomplished, this book will have outlived its usefulness and should have value only as a relic in the curious history of literary taste.

Let me begin, then, by using this notion of fabulation without defining it too precisely, using the fable of king and fabulator only as a point of departure, suggestive not definitive. In examining some aspects of the work of these exciting writers who have turned away from the realistic novel, my aim will be to discover what directions they are turning toward and to suggest what we as readers need in the way of equipment and expectations in order to acquire a taste for these strange new objects on the tree of narrative.

CHAPTER 2 FABULATION AS REVIVAL
OF ROMANCE

I LAWRENCE DURRELL AND THE RETURN
TO ALEXANDRIA

Once upon a time the first words of a story used to be
"Once upon a time." But these are the last words, or almost the last words, of Lawrence Durrell's *Alexandria
Quartet*. Which suggests that we may have come to the
end of a literary cycle, or rather to the beginning of a new
loop in the spiral of literary history. You remember the
passage which closes *Clea*, the last volume of the *Quartet*:

> Yes, one day I found myself writing down with trembling fingers
> the four words (four letters! four faces!) with which every story-
> teller since the world began has staked his slender claim to the
> attention of his fellow men. Words which presage simply the old
> story of an artist coming of age. I wrote: "Once upon a time . . ."
> And I felt as if the whole universe had given me a nudge!

In reading the passage we feel very strongly a kind of dual-
ity which pervades Durrell's work: we are pulled toward

the primitive by those four magical words and by the description of the artist as a mere story-teller, but we are also made aware of the modernity of the work; we are pulled toward the sophisticated by the preoccupation of the passage with the art of story-telling. Like so many modern works, this is a portrait of the artist, a *Künstlerroman*, about a character in a book who is writing a book in which he is a character. And the shades of Proust and Gide, among others, hover between our eyes and the page. What is new in Durrell, however, is neither the primitive nor the sophisticated but his peculiar combination of the two.

Take, for example, the scene in which Pursewarden and Justine visit the house of the child prostitutes. The two visitors are surrounded by these terrible children, who in another scene nearly drive Mountolive out of his wits as they attempt to capture him in the manner of the Lilliputians against Gulliver. Pursewarden describes the way Justine tames the little creatures:

> And when the light was brought she suddenly turned herself, crossed her legs under her, and in the ringing words of the street story-teller she intoned: "Now gather about me, all ye blessed of Allah, and hear the wonder of the story I shall tell you . . ."
> It was a wild sort of poetry for the place and the time—the little circle of wizened faces, the divan, the flopping light; and the strangely captivating lilt of the Arabic with its heavy damascened imagery, the thick brocade of alliterative repetitions, the nasal twanging accents, gave it a Laic splendour which brought tears to my eyes—gluttonous tears! It was such a rich diet for the soul! It made me aware how thin the fare is which we moderns supply to our hungry readers. The epic contours, that is what her story had. I was envious. How rich those beggar children were. And I was envious too of her audience. Talk of suspended judgment! They sank into the imagery of her story like plummets.

This scene is typical of the book. It is wild, exotic, romantic. Yet its main interest is not life, but art. It is really a little essay in esthetics, presented in the form of a dramatic scene. It reminds us of the moments in *Don Quixote* when there is a pause in the adventures of the Knight of the Mournful Countenance to allow for a literary discussion involving the Bachelor and the Curate or some passing stranger. And the resemblance is not a chance one. Cervantes's work was written as an anti-romance, and became, via Fielding and Smollett in English tradition, a major ancestor of a new literary form—the novel. Durrell's work, as the passage quoted above indicates, is an anti-novel in the same sense as Cervantes's work was an anti-romance. Both men were faced with a constricting literary tradition and revolted against it.

Of course, Pursewarden's point about the thinness of modern literary fare is not meant to be mere literary discussion in a vacuum, any more than the similar discussions in *Don Quixote*. We are meant to apply Pursewarden's theory to Durrell's practice. To do so we must look back, as Pursewarden suggests, to an older literary tradition than the novel. And so we shall. But before we do so we must observe that Durrell's revolt is not an isolated and magnificent gesture of defiance against an entrenched and flourishing literary tradition. The tradition he finds thin and constricting is the very one started by Cervantes—the tradition which begins as anti-romance and gradually insists on more and more scientific treatment of life: the empirical tradition which in its theoretical formulations calls itself first realism and finally naturalism. The naturalism to which Durrell is reacting is, of course, about as feeble now as the romances were in the time of Cervantes, and the new revolutionary is no more alone in his revolt than the old. A James Joyce can adapt naturalism to allegorical purposes as well as an Edmund Spenser could adapt romance. And a Marcel Proust can destroy empirical notions of characterization as thoroughly as Cervantes himself could destroy the romantic heroes. Just as Samuel Beckett is the heir of Joyce —a somewhat rebellious heir, producing anti-naturalistic anti-allegories—Lawrence Durrell is the heir of Proust. For it is Proust who explodes the empirical notions of characterization so essential to realistic and naturalistic fiction, by demonstrating the artificiality of the real and the reality of the artificial. "Even in the most insignificant details of our daily life," the narrator of *Swann's Way* tells us,

none of us can be said to constitute a material whole, which is identical for everyone, and need only be turned up like a page in an account book or the record of a will; our social personality is created by the thoughts of other people. Even the simple act which we describe as "seeing someone we know" is, to some extent, an intellectual process. We pack the physical outline of the creature we see with all the ideas we have already formed about him . . . so that each time we see the face or hear the voice it is our own ideas of him which we recognize and to which we listen.

Proust emphasizes here the artificiality of reality. We do not see our friends, only our ideas of them. In another passage he develops this paradox further, illustrating the converse principle, the reality of artifice:

None of the feelings which the joys or misfortunes of a "real" person awaken in us can be awakened except through a mental picture of those joys or misfortunes; and the ingenuity of the first novelist lay in his understanding that, as the picture was the one essential element in the complicated structure of our emotions, so, that simplification of it which consisted in the suppression, pure and simple, of "real" people would be a decided improvement. A real person, profoundly as we may sympathize with him, is in great measure perceptible only through our senses, that is to say, he remains opaque, offers a dead weight which our sensibilities have not the strength to lift. . . . The novelist's happy discovery was to think of substituting for those opaque sections, impenetrable by the human spirit, their equivalent in immaterial sections, things, that is, which the spirit can assimilate to itself.

Proust's brilliant exposition of the paradoxical notion that we can truly experience life only through art is the death knell of the realistic-naturalistic movement in fiction, though even today, forty years afterward, neo-naturalists like James Jones continue to write frantically, headless chickens unaware of the decapitating axe. For Durrell, however, Proust's new esthetic is a release and an inspiration. In the following passages from *Justine*, we can observe him adapting the Proustian view to his own purposes. In the first we find the narrator, Darley, examining Arnauti's diary, *Moeurs*, in which Justine is a character called Claudia:

Nor can it be said that the author's intentions are not full of interest. He maintains for example that real people can only exist in the imagination of an artist strong enough to contain them and give them form. "Life, the raw material, is only lived *in potentia* until the artist deploys it in his work. Would that I could do this service for poor Justine."

Like Pursewarden, Arnauti longs for a different kind of fiction. He wishes to set his ideal book "free to dream." His view is different from Pursewarden's but complementary, not contradictory; and Durrell's novel embodies both views. Darley finds Arnauti's diary so vivid that he feels at times like some paper character out of *Moeurs*. And after Pursewarden's death he writes of him,

How much of him can I claim to know? I realize that each person can only claim one aspect of our character as part of his knowledge.

To every one we turn a different face of the prism. Over and over again I have found myself surprised by observations which brought this home to me. . . . And as for Pursewarden, I remember, too, that in the very act of speaking . . . he straightened himself and caught sight of his pale reflection in the mirror. The glass was raised to his lips, and now, turning his head he squirted out upon his own glittering reflection a mouthful of the drink. That remains clearly in my mind: a reflection liquifying in the mirror of that shabby, expensive room which seems now so appropriate a place for the scene which must have followed later that night.

The *Alexandria Quartet* is alive with mirrors. The prismatic facets of character glitter, unreconciled, in our imaginations. Appearance and reality are continually confused, and the line between life and art continually blurred. Darley feels like a character out of *Moeurs*. But Darley *is* a character in Durrell's novel. What we took for fact in one volume is exposed as false in another, and the exposé itself is proved incorrect in the third. Stendhal could compare his story to a mirror, strolling down a lane, reflecting the sky and the mud. But for Durrell fiction is a whirling prism reflected in a liquifying mirror. In the scene quoted at the beginning of this chapter, in which Justine tells the child prostitutes a story in Arabic, Pursewarden longs for the opportunity to tell a story of Laic splendor to an audience which is really able to suspend its disbelief. Since the modern reader cannot recapture the esthetic innocence of Justine's audience, Durrell attempts on the one hand to establish in the reader's mind his version of the new, Proustian esthetic, and on the other to blur the line between the real and the artificial in order to make it harder for the reader to begin applying his disbelief, even if he refuses to suspend it. Durrell seeks to confuse and bewilder the reader, to separate him from his habitual reliance on probability and verisimilitude, so as to offer him something better. *Behold,* he as much as tells us, *you thought you could not walk without that crutch of realism. I tell you you can fly!* And he nearly convinces us that we can. Using the modern esthetic of Proust, and a narrative technique which, with its multiple narrators and dislocations of time, seems also typically modern, Durrell takes us on a journey—a magic carpet ride not only through space but through time as well—a return to Alexandria.

For, though Pursewarden says he longs for the old "epic contours," what Durrell gives us is—appropriately enough —more Alexandrian than Attic. As Moses Hadas has observed in his introduction to *Three Greek Romances,* " 'Once upon a time' is not the way the classical Greeks opened a work of literature." But "Once upon a time" does reflect the spirit of Alexandrian literature and of the romances written in the Greek language all over the Mediterranean world in post-Alexandrian times. Alexandria was a Greek city on Egyptian soil. In it the East and West met as they rarely have elsewhere. The old joke has it that when Greek meets Greek, they open a restaurant. But when Greek met Egyptian in ancient Alexandria, they opened a library. From this meeting of cultures developed the first literary critics and a new kind of literature. E. M. Forster has described this literature for us in his *Alexandria, a History and a Guide*—a book Lawrence Durrell frequently alludes to in the *Alexandria Quartet.* Forster points out that the distinguishing characteristic of the new literature was its emphasis on love:

Ancient Greece had also sung of love, but with restraint, regarding it as one activity among many. The Alexandrians seldom sang of anything else: their epigrams, their elegies and their idylls, their one great epic, all turn on the tender passion, and celebrate it in ways that previous ages had never known. . . .

> Who sculptured love and set him by the pool,
> Thinking with water such a fire to cool?

runs a couplet ascribed to one of the early Librarians, and containing in brief the characteristics of the school—decorative method, mythological allusiveness, and the theme of love.

How appropriate, too, that in the twentieth century Durrell's anti-novel should be set in this romantic spot. It is clear that Durrell's Alexandria is as much a country of the mind as Poe's Virginia or Kafka's Germany. Some of the place-names are real, but beyond that there is little resemblance between the fictional Alexandria of Durrell and the geographical one. Yet Durrell's work is completely faithful to the ancient spirit of the place.

As Forster points out, the literature of Alexandria was, unlike the literature of Greece itself, a literature of love. It was in Alexandria that love made its way into epic poetry: in the *Argonautica* of the librarian Apollonius the love of Medea for Jason was presented so dramatically that it left an indelible mark on poetic fiction. Vergil's Dido and many of Ovid's love-stricken females are directly derived from this Alexandrian epic. And the prose romances that were written in Greek around the Mediterranean in the second and third centuries A.D. (of which Heliodorus' *Ethiopica* and Longus' *Daphnis and Chloe* are the best known examples) are also derived, apparently, from the Alexandrian combination of Greek and Oriental literary traditions. A papyrus dating from the second century B.C. and called "The Alexandrian Erotic Fragment" was described by its last editor as being written in Greek prose similar to the ornate rhyming prose of Arabic narrative. In its combination of erotic subject matter and rich prose it also exemplifies the characteristic qualities of Durrell's work, written over two millennia later.

The *Ethiopica*, richest and most elaborate of the Greek romances, stands very much in the same relation to the Homeric epics as Durrell's *Quartet* does to such great realistic novels of the nineteenth century as *Anna Karenina* and *Middlemarch*. Both the epics and the great realistic novels present events as ordered by an omniscient narrator whose controlling mind not only shapes the events but colors them and comments on them. But in Heliodorus much of the narrative is conveyed to us directly by characters in the story. Furthermore, Heliodorus is not content simply to imitate the *Odyssey* and have one man narrate much of his own tale. In the *Ethiopica* we have as many narrators as in the *Alexandria Quartet*. Indeed, one of the first stories we are told, a brief resumé of her life by the heroine, turns out to be a tissue of falsehoods designed to deceive her captors (and also the reader, who only afterwards learns the truth). In the hands of Heliódorus the romance is characterized by a multiplicity of narrators and tales within tales like a sequence of Chinese boxes; by a consequent dislocation of the time scheme, as the narrative moves backwards and forwards from its beginning in what George Saintsbury has called a "sort of cat's cradle manner"; and by a fondness for elaborate set pieces of a spectacular nature, involving such things as battles, rituals, necromancy, and celebrations.

Though the general resemblance of the *Alexandria Quartet* to the *Ethiopica* is obvious (some of the action of the ancient story even takes place on the shores of Durrell's beloved Lake Mareotis), the point is not that the resemblance indicates any direct indebtedness; rather, it is that the two works are so similar in spirit. Durrell is not so much a descendant of Heliodorus as a reincarnation of him in the twentieth century. When Durrell speaks of his characters in an interview as "puppets," he reminds us of the way in which Heliodorus manipulates his characters in a virtuoso display of sustained and integrated form. And form, for Durrell, is nearly everything. His early novel, *The Black Book,* displays many of the characteristics of his later work—everything, almost, except form. *The Black Book* was written when Durrell was very much under the influence of D. H. Lawrence and Henry Miller, writers who tend to disdain form, to think of it as a way of distorting reality. In the recently published correspondence between Durrell and Miller we can see him gradually becoming more critical of Miller's work on the grounds of its formlessness. Though traces of Lawrence and Miller remain in Durrell's mature work, there can be little doubt that the spirit which presides over the *Alexandria Quartet* is Proust's. And in turning to Proust, Durrell brought himself into contact with a tradition of sustained form which was fundamentally opposed to the "slice of life" technique characteristic of empirically oriented mimetic fiction. The tradition of elaborate form in fiction leads back through the romances of the seventeenth century to the European rediscovery of Heliodorus in the sixteenth, whose influence on the subsequent development of prose fiction can hardly be exaggerated.

The purely melodramatic side of the Greek romance has, of course, been greatly modified in its modern reincarnation. In the old romances the characters were mainly highly stylized extremes of virtue and vice, and the plot was always subservient to the decorum of poetic justice. In the *Alexandria Quartet* the characters and the prevailing ethos are as elaborate and complicated as the plot and the setting. The thinness of characterization which, for the modern reader, relegates the *Ethiopica* to that secondary level of works whose influence surpasses their interest would be inexcusable in a modern work of serious intent. But even richness of characterization, which we think of as a peculiarly modern attribute of fiction, has its roots in Alexandria. The Alexandrians and their followers, especially Ovid and the Greek romancers, introduced the arts of rhetoric into narrative literature. The combination of psychology and rhetoric, which characterizes the crucial monologue of Medea in the Third Book of the *Argonautica*, works through Dido and the Ovidian lovers into the mainstream of narrative literature. Lawrence Durrell's rhetoric, rich and evocative as it is, has been roundly criticized by the English press as some sort of wild Celtic aberration—not (in the phrase of Mr. Podsnap) English, and hardly appropriate for a novel. But one of the glories of our resurgent narrative art has been the rhetoric of Joyce, of Faulkner, of Conrad, and of Proust; though none of them are (alas) English, either. The flat prose of sociological fiction is being abandoned to the sociologists, who, God knows, have need of it; and the rich rhetoric of the Alexandrians, of Ovid and the Greek romancers, is beginning once again to return narrative literature to the domain of art. The novel may indeed be dying, but we need not fear for the future. Durrell and others are generating a renaissance of romance. The return to Alexandria should be almost as exciting a voyage as the one described by the city's greatest story-teller, Apollonius; for, like the voyage of the

Argo, it will be an enchanted one. And already, like the laggard Argonauts on one occasion, we can hear our vehicle itself admonishing us:

> From Pelian Argo herself came a voice, bidding
> hasten away:
> For within her a beam divine had been laid, which
> Athena brought
> From the oak Dodonaean, and into the midst of
> her stem it was wrought.

II WHAT GOOD IS PURE ROMANCE?

A fair question, apparently. Plato asked it and nobody has answered it. Maybe it isn't as fair as it looks: what the question actually meant to him requires a bit of explanation. As I understand it, however, we can approximate Plato's intention by breaking the question into two parts: a) What good effect will listening to stories have on our understanding of the world?, and b) what good effect will listening to stories have on our behavior in the world? Like the good philosopher he was, Plato discovered that philosophy could do both a) and b) better than fiction could. That is, philosophy could tell us more truly both the nature of the cosmos and the attributes of right action. All those apologists for poetry who have accepted Plato's gambit have been reduced to presenting fiction either as sugar coating for the pill of philosophy, or as a handy and accurate shorthand notation of reality—that is, as allegory or as realism.

What Plato was really asking was "What good is poetry *as philosophy?*"—since for him philosophy already had a monopoly on both truth and goodness. Now that science owns truth and goodness knows where goodness went (religion had it last but seems to have mislaid it), Plato's question has shifted its meaning so far as to expose its underpinnings. Zola tried to answer the question, "What good is fiction *as science?*" and worked himself into the absurd corner of the "experimental" novel, a notion he seems to have had the good sense not to believe but merely to use as journalistic puffery for his own productions, much as his heirs are now crying "phenomenological" novel for similar reasons. Matthew Arnold tried to answer the question, "What good is fiction *as religion?*" and twisted himself around to the point where he could see literature replacing dogma. Now the Marxist asks, "What good is fiction *as politics?*," and the Freudian asks, "What good is fiction *as psychology?*," and so on. But the real question, the one that Plato pretended to be asking, has got lost. Probably Plato could not see it himself. Since literary criticism started as a branch of philosophy, it was doubtless necessary to see Plato's question in terms of metaphysics and ethics. Even Aristotle succeeded only in adding a psychological concept, *katharsis*, to his notion of literature, and then returned quickly to its philosophical value as "imitation." But now that we can see criticism as a branch of literature itself, we should be able to set Plato's question in its proper context and make it mean what it should mean: What are the special qualities of fiction for which we value it? In other words, "What good is fiction *as fiction?*"

Not as the "representation of an action" but as an imaginative construct. Not in terms of what it tells us about, even including the imagination itself, but in terms of what makes our experience of fiction a good experience. The Aristotle of *katharsis* is much closer to the mark than the

Aristotle of *mimesis*. The students of sleep have discovered that dreaming is necessary to the well-being of the human organism, and perhaps to the higher animals as well. It is not that our dreams teach us anything; they are simply a means of expression for us, a nightly cinema in which we are producer, director, all the actors, and all the audience. And if we are cheated of this imaginative performance in our sleep, we suffer for it during our waking existence in ways still not entirely understood.

I do not think fiction is a substitute for dream, but I think it must work for us in a similar way. It must provide us with an imaginative experience which is necessary to our imaginative well-being. And that is quite enough justification for it. We need all the imagination we have, and we need it exercised and in good condition. The simplest kind of fabling will do this for us to some extent, as long as we can respond to it fully, as long as it can engage our imagination totally. But as our imagination stretches and as we grow more serious (this combination of processes being what we mean, ideally, by the verb "to mature"), we require not fabling but fabulation. Pure romance must be enriched, like skim milk, if it is to sustain a full imaginative life. Allegory is one way of enriching pure romance. On this subject I shall have more to say later. Here, I want to point out only that there is a shadowy allegorical dimension to the *Alexandria Quartet* (an esthetic allegory, mainly, about ways of story-telling), and that this dimension is, in fact, part of the story.

But once this is said, it should be qualified by observing that Durrell's story is remarkably independent of its allegorical dimension. It is to the author's credit, I think, that he manages to be so engaging while keeping his narrative so squarely in the tradition of pure romance. He seems to have preserved enough from the tradition of the novel —to have learned enough from Lawrence, Proust, and others—to manage a revival of romance with a minimal amount of allegorizing. This is one important dimension of modern fabulation. In a way it is the simplest: the direct plunge back into the tide of story which rolls through all narrative art. Such a return to story for renewed vigor is a characteristic of the modern fabulators, though the others I am going to consider all add different qualities to their fabulations, which may tend to obscure the revival of romance in fabulation that Durrell exemplifies in so relatively pure a form. In the following two chapters, for example, I shall be examining certain ethical and psychological attitudes which give a special tone and meaning to much of modern fiction, a quality often vaguely referred to as "black humor." And in the next two after those, I shall be dealing with allegory, mainly. But I hope, in considering these other dimensions of fabulation, not to forget that of story, which is really the heart of the matter. Without it, the blood of narrative ceases to flow. The humors atrophy, the brain shrivels, and finally the soul itself departs.

CHAPTER 3 FABULATION AND SATIRE

I BLACK HUMOR

One of the most obvious and permanent qualities of the
fable proper—the little brother of the full-scale fabulations
we are considering—is that it has a moral. It is didactic. ←
Or so it seems until we look into the matter. In practice
we find that many collections of fables include some tales
without morals, and that in many other cases, well-mean-
ing souls have tacked morals onto tales for which they are
absurd or grossly inadequate. For instance, consider this
gem from a collection called *A C. Mery Talys* (*A Hundred
Merry Tales*, 1526—this is Paul Zall's modernized version
from his Bison paperback edition):

54.
   A young man of the age of 20 years, rude, and unlearned, in the
time of Lent came to his curate to be confessed—which, when he
was of his life searched and examined, could not say his Pater
Noster. Wherefore his confessor exhorted him to learn his Pater

Noster and showed him what an holy and goodly prayer it was and the effect thereof and the seven petitions therein contained:

"The first petition beginneth, Pater Noster, etc., that is to say— 'O Father hallowed by Thy name among men in earth as among angels in heaven.' The second, Adveniat, etc., 'Let Thy kingdom come and reign Thou among us men in earth as among angels in heaven.' The third, Fiat, etc., 'Make us to fulfill Thy will here in earth as Thy angels in heaven.' The fourth, Panem nostrum, etc., 'Give us our daily sustenance always and help us as we give and help them that have need of us.' The fifth, Dimitte, etc., 'Forgive us our sins done to Thee as we forgive them that trespass against us.' The sixth, Et ne nos, 'Let us not be overcome with evil temptation.' The seventh, Sed libera, etc., 'But deliver us from all evil— Amen.' "

And then his confessor after this exposition to him made, enjoined him in penance to fast every Friday on bread and water till he had his Pater Noster well and sufficiently learned.

This young man meekly accepting his penance so departed and came home to one of his companions and said to his fellow: "So it is that my ghostly father hath given me in penance to fast every Friday on bread and water till I can say my Pater Noster. Therefore I pray ye teach me my Pater Noster and, by my troth, I shall therefore teach thee a song of Robin Hood that shall be worth 20 of it."

By this tale ye may learn to know the effect of the holy prayer of the Pater Noster.

This propensity in the fable to point a moral at all costs has been parodied beautifully by Thurber in such tales as "The Unicorn in the Garden," with its splendid moral of "Don't count your boobies until they are hatched." But as readers of fables we can draw, if not a moral, at least a conclusion, from the existence of these two kinds of little fables—that is, the Aesopian kind where the moral really works, and those such as the one I quoted, which are essentially amoral and resist violently any attempt to assimilate them as exempla of an orderly moral world. The moral fable is kin to the larger satire; the amoral fable to the picaresque tale, which can grow very long indeed. And both of these large forms have something to do with that move-ment in modern fiction—in modern life, really, because it is not exclusively literary—which is often called Black Humor. Most of this country's exciting young writers are connected in some way with this literary movement. Albee, Barth, Donleavy, Friedman, Hawkes, Heller, Purdy, Pyn-chon, Southern and Vonnegut have all been stamped with this dark label at one time or another, and, various as the writings of these men actually are, their works differ from those of the previous generation in a manner special enough to justify some common terminology and some considera-tion of what their work, collectively, implies about the cur-rent literary situation. The term Black Humor is probably too clumsy to be of much use to criticism, but before dis-carding it we should do well to milk it of such value as it may have in helping us to understand this new fiction and to adjust to it. We can begin with a view from the inside:

They say it is a critic's phrase, Black Humor, and that whatever it is, you can count on it to fizzle after a bit. . . . I think they may be wrong on that . . . count. I have a hunch Black Humor has probably always been around, always will. . . .

The quotation is from Bruce Jay Friedman's shrewd and engaging foreword to an anthology, *Black Humor*, that he edited for Bantam Books in 1965. The anthology itself is worth looking at, as it includes work by a number of ex-citing writers, including Mr. Friedman himself. But it is not a really successful book, this anthology, mainly because some of the best Black Humorists tend to use larger forms than the short story, building effects over many pages.

Selections from Barth's *Sot-Weed Factor* and Heller's *Catch-22*, for example, hardly begin to work in this format.

But I don't mean to discuss Mr. Friedman's anthology here. I mention it because I want to use his definition as a point of departure for some theorizing of my own. Friedman suggests that we have a kind of Black Humor movement in contemporary writing because events "Out There" in the contemporary world are so absurd that the response of the Black Humorist is the most appropriate one possible. But he also suggests, in the lines just quoted, that Black Humor is not merely a modern fad but a continuing mode of literary activity. He doesn't say how this apparent contradiction is to be resolved, however, and this is where I want to begin. I think he is right on both counts. Black Humor is a modern movement but also a development in a continuing tradition.

Most of the literary kinds and modes are with us all the time, but in every era some are very alive and others quite dormant. If we consider literature as a way of looking at the world, for every age certain modes serve better than others to bring things into focus, to align the ideals of the age with actuality. In a historical perspective Black Humor seems allied with those periodic waves of rationality which have rolled through Western culture with continually increasing vigor for over two thousand years. The intellectual comedy of Aristophanes, the flourishing satire of imperial Rome, the humanistic allegories and anatomies of the later Middle Ages, the picaresque narratives of the Renaissance, the metaphysical poems and satires of the seventeenth century, and the great satiric fictions of the Age of Reason—all these are ancestors of modern Black Humor. Of course, an illustrious pedigree does not guarantee the worth of an offspring. Nevertheless, since understanding and evaluating depend so completely on our sense of genre, pedigree is where we must begin. This is especially important in the case of the so-called Black Humorists: first, because their immediate point of departure has been the novel, a form which we view with certain realistic expectations; and second, because nearly two centuries of literature dominated by romantic notions of value lie between the modern Black Humorists and such immediate ancestors as Swift and Voltaire.

Developments in current fiction are very closely analogous to the poetic revolution of a generation or so back, when the rediscovery of the metaphysical poets helped spark a revival of witty, cerebral verse. Current interest in Rabelais, Cervantes, Aleman, Grimmelshausen, Swift, Smollett, and Voltaire is part of the general drift of fiction into more violent and more intellectual channels. The sensibility and compassion which characterized the great novels of the nineteenth century are being modified by the wit and cruelty of Black Humor. Horace Walpole's epigram about life's being tragic for those who feel and comic for those who think is a gross oversimplification, no doubt, but it is useful to us in describing such a massive change in literary climate as the one we are considering here. Such changes, like variations in the weather, are not things one can do much to alter. The question is how to adjust to them.

For us, the question—like most literary questions—becomes one of how to read. What expectations should we bring to this new writing? What benefit can we hope to derive from it? To put it crudely, what's in it for us? I think there is a lot in it for us—it is our literature, speaking to us most immediately. If it seems out of focus, perhaps we must change our lenses to see it clearly. First of all, we must discard the notion that these works are "novels" as novels have been written. They are different from their immediate predecessors. Here the pedigree of Black Humor will help, for it is surely better to think of Voltaire and Swift when reading Vonnegut and Barth than to think of Hemingway and Fitzgerald. But we must not take the pedigree in too simple-minded a fashion either. If we say, "O yes, satire" we may go just as wrong as if we were to expect another realistic novel. Though these works are off-shoots of a family tree we recognize, they are a new muta-tion, a separate branch with its own special characteristics and qualities. To define the special attributes of this new branch is surely the critic's business. But it is a hard business because the writers are a mixed group, differing in tempera-ment, intellect, and experience; and because they them-selves are experimenting with this new uncrystallized mode of writing, often trying new things from book to book. A writer like John Hawkes seems almost to obliterate his hu-mor with his blackness, while Bruce Jay Friedman makes a nearly opposite emphasis. How can we unite such dis-parity other than by mere verbal trickery or sleight-of-word?

I am hedging here, warning the reader to take my at-tempt to define a revolution in progress as necessarily a tentative formulation. But despite the difficulty, I think enough can be said to justify the project. I see Black Hu-mor as crucially different from its satiric and picaresque ancestors, but also as clearly relatable to these two tradi-tional kinds of fiction. In this chapter and the following one I intend to explore certain aspects of these relation-

ships. First, the relationship of Kurt Vonnegut's kind of
Black Humor to the satirical tradition. Then, the relationship of Terry Southern and John Hawkes to the picaresque
tradition. This arrangement is not intended to be a neat
pigeonholing affair: for, first of all, in practice satire and
picaresque are often very hard to distinguish from one
another, and second, all three of these writers are clearly
inheritors of both traditions. I have divided the genres in
this manner mainly for convenience—but not arbitrarily,
as I hope to demonstrate.

The satirical kind of Black Humor is qualified by the
modern fabulator's tendency to be more playful and more
artful in construction than his predecessors: his tendency
to fabulate. Fabulative satire is less certain ethically but
more certain esthetically than traditional satire. This causes
the special tone that the phrase Black Humor so inade-
quately attempts to capture. The spirit of playfulness and
the care for form characteristic of the modern fabulators
operate so as to turn the materials of satire and protest
into comedy. And this is not a mere modern trick, a way-
ward eccentricity. These writers reflect quite properly their
heritage from the esthetic movement of the nineteenth
century and the ethical relativism of the twentieth. They
have some faith in art but they reject all ethical absolutes.
Especially, they reject the traditional satirist's faith in the
efficacy of satire as a reforming instrument. They have a
more subtle faith in the humanizing value of laughter.
Whatever changes they hope to work in their readers are
the admittedly evanescent changes inspired by art, which
need to be continually renewed, rather than the dramatic
renunciations of vice and folly postulated by traditional
satire.

The special tone of Black Humor, often derived from presenting the materials of satire in a comic perspective, is perfectly illustrated in a passage from Vonnegut's *Cat's Cradle*. The narrator in this passage is interviewing the son of a Schweitzer-type jungle doctor on a small Caribbean island:

"Well, aren't you at all tempted to do with your life what your father's done with his?"

Young Castle smiled wanly, avoiding a direct answer. "He's a funny person, Father is," he said, "I think you'll like him."

"I expect to. There aren't many people who've been as unselfish as he has."

"One time," said Castle, "when I was about fifteen, there was a mutiny near here on a Greek ship bound from Hong Kong to Havana with a load of wicker furniture. The mutineers got control of the ship, didn't know how to run her, and smashed her up on the rocks near 'Papa' Monzano's castle. Everybody drowned but the rats. The rats and the wicker furniture came ashore."

That seemed to be the end of the story, but I couldn't be sure. "So?"

"So some people got free furniture and some people got bubonic plague. At Father's hospital, we had fourteen hundred deaths inside of ten days. Have you ever seen anyone die of bubonic plague?"

"That unhappiness has not been mine."

"The lymph glands in the groin and the armpits swell to the size of grapefruit."

"I can well believe it."

"After death, the body turns black—coals to Newcastle in the case of San Lorenzo. When the plague was having everything its own way, the House of Hope and Mercy in the Jungle looked like Auschwitz or Buchenwald. We had stacks of dead so deep and wide that a bulldozer actually stalled trying to shove them toward a common grave. Father worked without sleep for days, worked not only without sleep but without saving many lives, either."

[*After an interruption*]

"Well, finish your story anyway."

"Where was I?"

"The bubonic plague. The bulldozer was stalled by corpses."

"Oh, yes. Anyway, one sleepless night I stayed up with Father while he worked. It was all we could do to find a live patient to treat. In bed after bed after bed we found dead people.

"And Father started giggling," Castle continued.

"He couldn't stop. He walked out into the night with his flashlight. He was still giggling. He was making the flashlight beam dance over all the dead people stacked outside. He put his hand on my head, and do you know what that marvelous man said to me?" asked Castle.

"Nope."

" 'Son,' my father said to me, 'someday this will all be yours.' "

In the passage an excess of the horrible is faced and defeated by the only friend reason can rely on in such cases: laughter. The whole episode is a comic parable of our times. Progress, that favorite prey of satirists from Swift and Voltaire onward, means that some people get free furniture and some get the plague. Some get Biarritz and some get Auschwitz. Some get cured of cancer by radiation; others get radiation sickness. But the spuriousness of progress is not seen here with the *saeva indignatio* of the satirist. Progress is seen not as a conspiracy but as a joke. The Black Humorist is not concerned with what to do about life but with how to take it. In this respect Black Humor has certain affinities with some existentialist attitudes, roughly distinguishable in terms of the difference between seeing the universe as absurd and seeing it as ridiculous—a joke. The absurd universe is a pretty dismal affair. The best, in fact, that Camus found to offer humanity as a response to the human condition was "scorn." In "The Myth of Sisyphus" he told us that "there is no fate that

cannot be surmounted by scorn." The Black Humorists
offer us something better than scorn. They offer us laughter.
The scorn of Sisyphus leads finally to resignation—"He,
too, concludes that all is well." Beneath the hide of this
scornful hero beats the heart of Dr. Pangloss after all.
Vonnegut's fictional prophet Bokonon suggests a better
posture for man on the mountain top than that of Camus's
Sisyphus, who simply starts down again to pick up his
burden. At the end of Cat's Cradle, with the world nearly
all frozen, Bokonon gives one of his last disciples a bit of
advice:

> If I were a younger man, I would write a history of human stu-
> pidity; and I would climb to the top of Mount McCabe and lie
> down on my back with my history for a pillow; and I would take
> from the ground some of the blue-white poison that makes statues
> of men; and I would make a statue of myself, lying on my back,
> grinning horribly, and thumbing my nose at You Know Who.

What man must learn is neither scorn nor resignation,
say the Black Humorists, but how to take a joke. How
should one take a joke? The best response is neither acquiescence nor bitterness. It is first of all a matter of perception. One must "get" the joke. Then one must demonstrate this awareness by playing one's role in the joke in
such a way as to turn the humor back on the joker or cause
it to diffuse itself harmlessly on the whole group which
has participated in the process of the joke. Even at the
punch line of apocalypse, feeble man can respond with the
gesture prescribed by Bokonon, suggesting an amused, tol-
erant defiance. Of course, a joke implies a Joker, as Glouces-
ter observed amid the cosmic tomfoolery of King Lear:
"They kill us for their sport." But I do not think the Black
Humorists mean to present us with a new deity, crowned

with a cap and bells in place of thorns. No more than Paul Tillich do they wish to "bring in God as a *deus ex machina*" to fill the great hole in the modern cosmos. To see the human situation as a cosmic joke, one need not assume a Joker.

Some accidents are so like jokes that the two are indistinguishable. Moreover, it is possible to conceive of all human history as part of a master plan without thinking of the Planner in quite the traditional way. In an early science fiction novel, now re-released in paperback, Kurt Vonnegut developed such a view. In *Sirens of Titan* he presented a cosmos in which the whole of human history has been arranged by intervention from outer space in order to provide a traveler from a distant galaxy with a small spare part necessary for his craft to continue its voyage to the other side of the universe. Such purposefulness to entirely extra-human ends is indeed a cosmic joke, but is not intended as such by those superior beings who have manipulated earthly life for their own ends. This novel suggests that the joke is on us every time we attribute purpose or meaning that suits us to things which are either accidental, or possessed of purpose and meaning quite different from those we would supply. And it doesn't matter which of these mistakes we make.

Samuel Johnson, whose *Rasselas* is a rather solemn ancestor of *Cat's Cradle*, picked on just this aspect of the vanity of human wishes in one of his finest works—an *Idler* paper so black and humorous that Johnson later suppressed it. In this essay Johnson presented a dialogue between a mother vulture and her children, in which the wise old bird, looking down at a scene of human carnage from a recent European battle, tells her young that men do this at regular intervals as part of a divine plan which has shaped the best of all possible worlds—for vultures. In presenting this view of life as a joke on all those who think this is the best of all possible worlds for men, Johnson is very close to his modern descendants. For the joke is one key to the fabulative impulse, especially to the impulse behind Black Humor. To present life as a joke is a way of both acknowledging its absurdity and showing how that very absurdity can be encompassed by the human desire for form. A joke like Dr. Johnson's acknowledges and counteracts the pain of human existence. In the best of all possible worlds there would be no jokes.

Of all the things that men must endure, war is one of the worst. Certainly war brings the contrast between human ideals and human actions to the highest possible degree of visibility. In time of war the drums, the rituals, the rhetoric all collaborate to suppress reason and its ally laughter, to prevent any rational scrutiny of such an irrational process. But satirists and picaresque novelists have subjected these phenomena to their fierce scrutiny nonetheless. Grimmelshausen's *Simplicissimus* is an honored ancestor of Céline's *Journey to the End of Night,* and the king of Brobdingnag's pronouncement on European history still reverberates in our ears with an eerie relevance to modern conditions. The Black Humorists of today, of course, have found the fields of Mars as fertile as ever. *Catch-22* and *Dr. Strangelove* are among the triumphs of modern comic fiction. Thus it should not surprise us to find that two of Kurt Vonnegut's strongest performances deal with modern war: one with World War II, and one with the scientific discovery of an ultimate weapon.

II "CAT'S CRADLE" AND "MOTHER NIGHT"

These two works will serve well to indicate the r
quality of Vonnegut's achievement to date and also will
help to reinforce the distinction I have been trying to make
between the modern fabulator's comedy of extremity and
the method of traditional satire. The need to insist on this
distinction is demonstrated continually, but I can illustrate
it by citing a retrospective review of Vonnegut's work which
appeared in the *New Republic* between the time when I
wrote most of this chapter and the moment I am writing
these words:

And so goes Vonnegut's most powerful writing. All the anger, the
shame, the shock, the guilt, the compassion, the irony, the control
to produce great satire are *there*. . . . Why, then, does Vonnegut
settle for such lovely, literate amusing attacks upon such simple
targets as scientists, engineers, computer technicians, religion, the
American Legion, artists, company picnics?

These words are a comment on a passage from the introduction to *Mother Night*, which will be quoted below, but
they are meant as a reaction to all of Vonnegut's work, and
could serve as a typical reaction to much of Black Humor.
The review from which I have taken this criticism is long
and favorable, but the reviewer is finally baffled by Vonnegut's refusal to turn his material into satire. Such a reaction, it seems to me, is clearly better than assuming either
that Vonnegut has produced works of satire or that he is
trying to and failing. But it is still an unfortunate reaction
and, in a word, wrong. It is based, I should judge, on the
assumption that satire is "better" than comedy. Why any-

one should assume this, I do not know, though I suspect such an assumption goes along with a belief that the world is sick and the satirist can cure it by rubbing its nose in the filth it produces. This assumption is one that I want to reject. The world, in any fair historical perspective, is about as sick or healthy as it has been. These times are perhaps more dangerous than some moments in the past, because man's weapons are stronger, but that goes for his weapons against disease as well as for his weapons against life. But whether the world is especially sick, now, or not, there is no evidence that satire ever cured any human ailment, or any social disease either. In fact the whole notion of "great satire" seems rather suspect from this point of view. What *are* the great satires? And what are the hard targets they attack? Is Dr. Pangloss a hard target? Or Stalinist Communism? Even Jonathan Swift's finest achievement, the fourth book of *Gulliver's Travels*, is hard to call a great satire, precisely because its greatness is problematic and not satiric at all.

If I tried to pin down the nature of Vonnegut's fabulation—to find a phrase more descriptive than Black Humor and more precise—I would, borrowing a phrase Hugh Kenner used in another connection, call Vonnegut's work stoical comedy. Or perhaps I would go one step further and call it Epicurean comedy—if I could take my definition of Epicureanism from Walter Pater's elaborate fabulation on that subject. Like Pater's *Marius*, Vonnegut's works exhibit an affection for this world and a desire to improve it—but not much hope for improvement. (In making this suggestion toward a name for Vonnegut's fabulation, I do not mean to suggest that it resembles Pater's work in any respect. The slow, dreamy movement of *Marius* is a far cry from Vonnegut's crisp deftness. If we can call Vonnegut's work Epicurean comedy, let us be sure to put the emphasis on the noun—he is a comic artist first and last.)

In *Cat's Cradle* Vonnegut brings his comic perspective to bear on contemporary aspects of the old collision between science and religion. The book is dominated by two characters who are offstage for the most part: a brilliant scientist and the founder of a new religion. The scientist, "Nobel prize physicist Felix Hoenikker," is presented as a child-like innocent who is finally as amoral as only an innocent child can be. He is a "father" of the atomic bomb (rather more of a father to it than to his three children) and he finally develops a much more potent device—*ice-nine*—which can (and does) freeze all the liquid on this watery globe. One of his children tells the narrator this anecdote about him:

> For instance, do you know the story about Father on the day they first tested a bomb out at Alamagordo? After the thing went off, after it was a sure thing that America could wipe out a city with just one bomb, a scientist turned to Father and said, "Science has now known sin." And do you know what Father said? He said, "What is sin?"

This anecdote parallels that told of the jungle doctor by *his* son, which I quoted earlier. The contrast between the aware humanity of the one and the terrible innocence of the other is pointed up by the parallel structure of the anecdotes. The doctor, however, is a minor figure, almost eclipsed by the major opposition between the sinless scientist and the distinctly fallen religious prophet, Bokonon. As the scientist finds the truth that kills, the prophet looks for a saving lie. On the title page of the first of the *Books of Bokonon*, the bible of this new religion, is the abrupt warning: "Don't be a fool! Close this book at once! It is nothing but *foma!*" *Foma* are lies. Bokonon, a Negro from Tobago in the Caribbean, has invented a religion for the island of San Lorenzo (where he arrived, a castaway, after considerable experience of the world). His "Bible" includes some parable-like anecdotes, some epigrams, and many psalm-like calypsos, such as this one:

> I wanted all things
> To seem to make some sense,
> So we all could be happy, yes,
> Instead of tense.
> And I made up lies
> So that they all fit nice,
> And I made this sad world
> A par-a-dise.

The epigraph to Vonnegut's book reads this way:

> Nothing in this book is true.
> "Live by the *foma* * that make you brave and
> kind and healthy and happy."
>
> *The Books of Bokonon.* 1:5
> * harmless untruths

The author's disclaimer is partly a parody of the usual "any resemblance to actual persons . . ." hedge against libel suits. But it is also a way of encircling Bokononism and making *Cat's Cradle* a repository of religious untruth itself. The very confrontation in the book between science and religion is aimed at developing the "cruel paradox" that lies at the center of Bokononist thought as it lies at the center of our world: "the heartbreaking necessity of lying about reality, and the heartbreaking impossibility of lying about it."

The ideas I have been trying to sketch out briefly here are only the string for Vonnegut's cat's cradle. The life of the book is in its movement, the turns of plot, of character, and of phrase which give it vitality. Vonnegut's prose has the same virtues as his characterization and plotting. It is deceptively simple, suggestive of the ordinary, but capable of startling and illuminating twists and turns. He uses the rhetorical potential of the short sentence and short paragraph better than anyone now writing, often getting a rich comic or dramatic effect by isolating a single sentence in a separate paragraph or excerpting a phrase from context for a bizarre chapter-heading. The apparent simplicity and ordinariness of his writing mask its efficient power, so that we are often startled when Vonnegut pounces on a tired platitude or cliché like a benevolent mongoose and shakes new life into it: "Son . . . someday this will all be yours."

Despite his mastery of the prose medium, and a sense of the ridiculous which is always on duty, Vonnegut never abandons himself to relentless verbal cleverness of the Peter De Vries sort. Sometimes we may wrongly suspect him of this kind of self-indulgence, as in the opening sentence of Cat's Cradle—"Call me Jonah"—which seems like a gratuitous though delightful parody of the opening of Moby Dick, until we realize that by invoking Jonah and his whale, along with the biblical Leviathan, Vonnegut is preparing us for a story on the Job theme, with the anti-Joblike conclusion provided by Bokonon's advice to the narrator on the proper posture for death in response to the plague of ice-nine (quoted on p. 44 above).

Vonnegut's prose always serves his vision and helps to make narrative structures of that vision. This process is illustrated nicely by a longish passage from the introduction he wrote in 1966 for the new edition of Mother Night. In it he speaks of his actual experience as a prisoner of war in Dresden, in prose which has the lucidity of the best journalism enriched with the poetic resources of a born storyteller. (One falls naturally into the word "speaks" in discussing this prose, which gives a strong sense of a voice behind the words.)

There were about a hundred of us in our particular work group, and we were put out as contract labor to a factory that was making a vitamin-enriched malt syrup for pregnant women. It tasted like thin honey laced with hickory smoke. It was good. I wish I had some right now. And the city was lovely, highly ornamented, like Paris, and untouched by war. It was supposedly an "open" city, not to be attacked since there were no troop concentrations or war industries there.

But high explosives were dropped on Dresden by American and British planes on the night of February 13, 1945, just about twenty-one years ago, as I now write. There were no particular targets for the bombs. The hope was that they would create a lot of kindling and drive firemen underground.

And then hundreds of thousands of tiny incendiaries were scattered over the kindling, like seeds on freshly turned loam. More bombs were dropped to keep firemen in their holes, and all the little fires grew, joined one another, became one apocalyptic flame. Hey presto: fire storm. It was the largest massacre in European history, by the way. And so what?

We didn't get to see the fire storm. We were in a cool meat-locker under a slaughterhouse with our six guards and ranks and ranks of dressed cadavers of cattle, pigs, horses, and sheep. We heard the bombs walking around up there. Now and then there would be a gentle shower of calcimine. If we had gone above to take a look, we would have been turned into artifacts characteristic of fire storms: seeming pieces of charred firewood two or three feet long—ridiculously small human beings, or jumbo fried grasshoppers, if you will.

The malt syrup factory was gone. Everything was gone but the cellars where 135,000 Hansels and Gretels had been baked like gingerbread men. So we were put to work as corpse miners, break-ing into shelters, bringing bodies out. And I got to see many Ger-man types of all ages as death had found them, usually with valu-ables in their laps. Sometimes relatives would come to watch us dig. They were interesting, too.

So much for Nazis and me.

If I'd been born in Germany, I suppose I would have *been* a Nazi, bopping Jews and gypsies and Poles around, leaving boots sticking out of snowbanks, warming myself with my secretly vir-tuous insides. So it goes.

The admission at the end of this passage suggests one rea-son why Vonnegut and other Black Humorists write the way they do. And in this respect they are close to the traditional satirists. They would like to prevent us from "warming ourselves with our secretly virtuous insides" while we condone the freezing of others. And as long as we per-sist in fire-bombing other human beings they would like to blow our cool for us. Comically but relentlessly they seek to make us thoughtful—in all the senses of that most sensi-ble word.

Mother Night is the autobiography of a fictional hero/criminal of World War II, Howard W. Campbell, Jr. This Campbell is a hero or criminal depending on how one looks at him. He is an American who stayed in Germany during the war to broadcast for the Nazis a special line of virulent anti-semitism and other hateful stuff: a Nazi hero, an American traitor. But in his broadcasts he was secretly sending back coded messages for American intelligence: an American hero, a Nazi traitor. The novel begins with Campbell in prison—"a nice new jail in old Jerusalem" —awaiting trial along with Adolph Eichmann. As Camp-bell unravels his life story we begin to find out how he got there and to worry about what will happen to him. These affairs are managed very skillfully. With perfect aplomb, Vonnegut juggles three distinct time schemes: the present, the past of the war period, and the past of the post-war period; and three distinct settings: Israel, Germany, and New York. The effect of this juggling is superbly controlled. It operates not so as to call attention to the juggler himself but so as to combine the narrative suspense involved in resolving these actions with a moral and intellectual suspense generated by them. From *what* and *how* we progress to *why* and *why not*—but without ceasing to care about *what* and *how*. I am not going to give away the lines of narrative development here. The reader deserves the pleasure of experiencing them firsthand, without warning. But I will give away one of the morals because Vonnegut himself mentions it in the first paragraph of his new introduction:

This is the only story of mine whose moral I know. I don't think it is a marvelous moral; I simply happen to know what it is: We are what we pretend to be, so we must be careful about what we pretend to be.

In Vonnegut, as in his contemporaries, we do not find the rhetoric of moral certainty, which has generally been a distinguishing characteristic of the satirical tradition. The writers of modern dark comedy do not seek the superior position of the traditional moralists. Nor do they point to other times and customs as repositories of moral values, or to any traditional system as The Law. Even in essaying to abstract a moral from his own book, Vonnegut makes no special claim for its virtues, or his. The book itself must be the test. Our experience of it must be satisfying and healthy. If this is so, then it may nourish our consciences without requiring reduction to a formula. My feeling is that, far from manifesting sickness (as some critics seem to feel it does), Black Humor is a sign of life and health.

Vonnegut, in his fiction, is doing what the most serious writers always do. He is helping, in Joyce's phrase, "to create the conscience of the race." What race? Human certainly, not American or German or any other abstraction from humanity. Just as pure romance provides us with necessary psychic exercise, intellectual comedy like Vonnegut's offers us moral stimulation—not fixed ethical positions which we can complacently assume, but such thoughts as exercise our consciences and help us keep our humanity in shape, ready to respond to the humanity of others.

4 FABULATION AND PICARESQUE

I BLACK HUMOR IN HAWKES AND SOUTHERN

John Hawkes is perhaps the most consciously traditional of all the modern fabulators. He is also the most experimental, the most *avant-garde*. I suspect this is no coincidence, and I take it as confirmation of my suspicion that when asked by the late John Enck whether he was an *avant-garde* writer, Hawkes replied in terms of tradition:

> My own concept of "avant-garde" has to do with something constant which we find running through prose fiction from Quevedo, the Spanish picaresque writer, and Thomas Nashe at the beginnings of the English novel, down through Lautréamont, Céline, Nathanael West, Flannery O'Connor, James Purdy, Joseph Heller, myself. This constant is a quality of coldness, detachment, ruthless determination to face up to the enormities of ugliness and potential failure within ourselves and in the world around us, and to bring to this exposure a savage or saving comic spirit and the saving beauties of language. . . . A writer who truly and greatly sustains us is Nabokov.

59

The line traced by Hawkes, here, from Spanish picaresque through French surrealism to such modern fabulators of the last generation as West and O'Connor is first of all a perfect piece of literary genealogy by a writer who sees his own family tree as clearly as the most gifted of critical heralds could hope to. And, unlike most writers, Hawkes has no desire to conceal—from himself or anyone else—his true ancestry. This may be because his work remains so unequivocally his own. As he put it in the same interview, discussing the one writer whose name really needs to be added to complete a Hawkesian genealogy,

as a matter of fact, while I was reading from *The Lime Twig* last night, I became quite conscious again of echoes of a Faulknerian use of inner consciousness and expanded prose rhythms. The echoes are undeniable, I think—Faulkner is still the American writer I most admire—though at this point I ought to insist again that my work is my own, and that my language, attitudes, and conceptions are unique.

In speaking thus of the writers he admires, Hawkes has not only traced for us his own literary pedigree, he has also pointed to one of the principal strands in the fabric of modern fabulation. In Durrell we saw the romantic strand, enriched by techniques learned from the novelists, but aiming at a return to the source of all fiction, the marvelous well-spring of pure story. In Vonnegut we saw the satiric strand, tempered by modern Epicureanism to a dark comedy of ideas. In Hawkes we have the picaresque strand, with its traditional cruelty and violence modified by its passage from a proto-realistic form to a surrealistic one. In this line of development Céline is a crucial figure and his *Journey to the End of Night* a crucial book. This work is so important because in it Céline seemed to recognize, more deeply than anyone before him, a natural tendency in picaresque toward a grotesque exaggeration of misfortunes: an intensification of everyday troubles into an ironic vision of a distorted cosmos, where a poetic injustice reigns, which destroys all who do not learn to accommodate themselves to it. Céline's surrealism gets to the black heart of the picaresque tradition and finds there an existential despair of the human condition as far removed from satire in one direction as the stoical or Epicurean comedy of Vonnegut is in the other. Content with this discovery, Céline preserved virtually intact the loose and episodic picaresque form which allowed his despairing imagination such freedom as it needed to range from scene to scene and topic to topic. From this point in the picaresque/surrealistic tradition, modern fabulation departs in a number of directions: some writers (and I would number Heller, in *Catch-22*, and Hawkes among them) move toward a tighter narrative structure; Purdy (in *Malcolm*) toward allegory; Terry Southern toward what we might call revenge comedy.

Such distinctions may seem like arid pedantry, but I want to insist on them. That term "Black Humor," which can be helpful up to a point, also tends to obscure both minor generic differences and the individual qualities of particular writers, leading us to such positions as an insistence that since Hawkes and Vonnegut are both doing Black Humor and doing it differently, then one must be right and the other wrong. To avoid this sort of critical absurdity we must resist such lumping in some way. The only legitimate way to approach "intention" in a literary work is through a highly discriminated sense of genre. Our reactions to such an immediately enjoyable and "popular" work as Terry Southern's *The Magic Christian*, even, will inevitably be enhanced if we are able to "place" the work in some way—if we are able, quite literally, to "get with it."

The Magic Christian has the loosest of narrative structures. It is truly episodic, in some ways resembling a rudimentary ancestor of picaresque more than picaresque itself. In its fundamental narrative pattern The Magic Christian is like those Renaissance jest books which string a sequence of quite separate practical jokes and witty replies on a thread consisting of a single central character: the merry pranks of Till Eulenspiegel or his English descendant Howleglass. There was a touch of Robin Hood in Howleglass, in that most of his pranks were directed at people of some substance or authority, but Guy Grand is fabulously rich and enjoys "making it hot" for rich and poor with equal vigor. He is no Robin Hood. What, then, is he? If The Magic Christian were an attack on anything, it would be an attack on the human condition. (I avoid the term "human nature" for the same reason the existentialists do. Southern is not satirizing man for his weaknesses. The object of his attention is not a string of human frailties such as the seven deadly sins. It is the total situation which makes for those forms of behavior which at one point in man's history seemed adequately described by the notion of seven deadly sins.) As I said, if this book were an attack, the human condition would be its object. But it is not an attack. Southern's attitude is beyond satire. It reminds us of H. L. Mencken's attitude toward the United States. Mencken's harshest criticisms of American life were always balanced by his feeling that such a rare zoo provided much too amusing a spectacle to abandon merely because it was a bit nauseating. Some such combination of horror and

amusement at American life must lie behind all of Southern's work—even the pornoparodical *Candy* and the peace-
nikky *Dr. Strangelove.* The traditional satirist is always
in the awkward position (for an artist) of trying to obliterate his material. If things or people really change he
will have to write something else. But there is in picaresque
fiction—from its earliest beginnings—a special relish for
the grotesque details of contemporary life and an appreciation of the fact that there is always a catch; which makes
its tone rueful but not revolutionary. The satirist often has
his vision of Utopia. The picaresque writer expects that
there will be catches even there.

The hero of Thomas Nashe's sixteenth-century quasi-
picaresque tale, *The Unfortunate Traveller,* thinks of himself on occasion as a divinely appointed minister of justice:
"I think confidently I was ordained God's scourge from
above." So does Hamlet think of himself at times, for that
matter, and so do most revengers in early fiction and
drama. The central character in *The Magic Christian,* Guy
Grand, who seems partly to be designated by the title
(which also refers to an ocean liner, the *S.S. Magic Christian*), is a scourge. He goes around "making it hot" for
people, playing somewhat the role assigned to devils in
Christian tradition. Like Satan, he is tempter and punisher,
and the righteous (or those who feel righteous) must take
pleasure in his actions. Thus, in this story Southern not
only distorts satiric materials into a comedy of excess, he
also imposes on the picaresque world an unlovable but
effective kind of poetic justice, which adds another dimension to the comedy—a Dantesque dimension. But the in-
habitants of Southern's inferno are not full-blooded sinners

paying the penalty for their willful crimes against God's law. They are automata, governed by stock-responses to various stimuli—mainly economic.

The man who behaves with rigid, mechanical actions in a world where most men act with some spontaneity is the archetype of the comic figure, Bergson tells us. But what happens when the world turns mechanical and all men behave according to banal and predictable patterns? Guy Grand, a sadist with a sense of humor, is the only "free" individual in the world of *The Magic Christian*—the only "individual" in fact. If we were truly automated ourselves, his actions could not amuse us. The fact that they do suggests that things are not completely hopeless. The mirror is distorted after all. One tiny episode, one of the least amusing in the book but handy because of its brevity, may serve as an example of Southern's technique of vengeful comic distortion:

Speaking of upsets though, Grand upset the equilibrium of a rather smart Madison Avenue advertising agency, Jonathan Reynolds, Ltd., by secretly buying it—*en passant*, so to speak—and putting in as president a pygmy.

At that time it was rare for a man of this skin-pigmentation or stature (much the less both) to hold down a top-power post in one of these swank agencies, and these two handicaps would have been difficult to overcome—though perhaps could have been overcome in due time had the chap shown a reasonable amount of savior-faire and general ability, or the promise of developing it. In this case, however, Grand had apparently paid the man to behave in an eccentric manner—to scurry about the offices like a squirrel and to chatter raucously in his native tongue. It was more than a nuisance.

An account executive, for example, might be entertaining an extremely important client in his own office, a little tête-à-tête of the very first seriousness—perhaps with an emissary of one of the soap-flake kings—when the door would burst open and in would fly the president, scrambling across the room and under the desk, shrieking pure gibberish, and then out he'd go again, scuttling crabwise over the carpet, teeth and eyes blazing.

"What in God's name was that?" the client would ask, looking slowly about, his face pocked with a terrible frown.

"Why, that . . . that . . ." But the a.e. could not bring himself to tell, not after the first few times anyway. Evidently it was a matter of pride.

Later this a.e. might run into one of his friends from another agency, and the friend would greet him:

"Say, hear you've got a new number one over at J.R., Tommy—what's the chap like?"

"Well, as a matter of fact, Bert . . ."

"You don't mean the old boy's got you on the *mat* already, Tommy. Ha-ha. *That* what you're trying to say?"

"No, Bert, it's . . . well I don't know, Bert, I *just don't know.*"

It was a matter of pride, of course. As against it, salaries had been given a fairly stiff boost, *and* titles. If these dapper execs were to go to another agency now, it would be at a considerable loss of dollars and cents. Most of the old-timers—and the younger ones too, actually—had what it took to stick it out there at J.R.

Like most of the book this episode draws some of its strength from the validity contained within its distortion. The flabby quality of American life, and in particular our tendency to respond automatically to economic stimuli and the pressures of status, are certainly being illustrated here. But they are not being satirized so much as chastised. Criticism and punishment are so closely fused in this episode that no residue of indignation remains when it is over. The pygmy punishes the venality of the flacks who work at Jonathan Reynolds even as he exposes that venality. And the flacks accept their lot—titles and fat paychecks in return for a purposeless and degrading existence. They "had what it took to stick it out there at J.R." What it took, of course, was "pride of status without pride in function" (Lionel Trilling's phrase)—an empty snobbery which one rejoices to see taking its appropriate punishment.

As I suggested earlier, the title seems to point in part to Guy Grand himself, whose penchant for making things hot for people suggests a devilish figure doing God's work of punishment in a wicked world. The whole book flirts with allegory of this sort. Even the pygmy episode is readily interpretable as a view of an affluent society, a prosperous but aimless state where everyone is well enough paid not to care about the direction of the enterprise. Or this same episode may be seen as an even grander scheme: a cosmic vision of a world which worships a figurehead divinity who talks gibberish while fronting for a real power concerned only with amusing itself at the expense of its creatures. Are such interpretations in the work or in us? It is hard to say. Southern seems to invite them, and in some episodes, like the voyage of the S.S. *Magic Christian*, he becomes more insistent. The whole question of allegory—and mock allegory or pseudo-allegory—is one which no treatment of modern fabulation can afford to ignore. Along with romance, satire, and picaresque, allegory is an important mode of fabulation—so important that it will be the principal subject of the next chapter. But now we must return to a consideration of picaresque elements in fabulation and to the work of John Hawkes in particular.

II JOHN HAWKES'S THEORY OF FICTION

Considering Hawkes as a picaresque writer, we can begin with the obvious fact that his affinities with the picaresque tradition are not mainly formal. He has accepted some of the dark premises of the picaresque attitude, but he has moved very far indeed from the loose and episodic picaresque form, with its simple, chronological string of events in the life of a roguish individual. In addition to Céline and the early picaresque writers, Hawkes admires Nathanael West, Flannery O'Connor, Faulkner, and Nabokov. His admiration for the last two, in particular, suggests the kind of delight in formal and verbal dexterity that is the essence of fabulation. For a modern writer, such care for form almost inevitably involves the rejection of any too easy adoption of the forms of his predecessors. Alain Robbe-Grillet, for example, in defending himself against charges that his writing is a kind of empty formalism, has responded with a counter-charge that the imitators of Balzacian realism are the true formalists because they slavishly copy the forms devised in another era by another sensibility to represent another reality. The artist who wants to capture modern life, this argument runs, must care for form, because only appropriately new forms will be capable of representing contemporary life. This is a powerful argument, though it does not guarantee that every experiment will succeed. Still less does it convince us that experiment and success are really the same thing. But it does put the argument for newness about as strongly as it can be put. Literary forms have a way of becoming stereotyped, especially successful ones, as anyone can tell who looks through the dreary history of "popular" English fiction. The novelists of the third rank and lower imitated their betters in much the same way that commercial television shows imitate a successful formula.

In the twentieth century it has become increasingly apparent that realism itself, instead of being simply the truest reflection of the world, was simply a formal device like any other, a tool to be put aside when it had lost its cutting edge. In making their revolt against the realistic novel, different writers have resorted to different stratagems. Some have paid lip service to realistic premises while calmly going their own way. Others have taken up polemical positions and publicly challenged representatives of the Old Guard. This latter method is more characteristic of the new French novelists than of their English and American counterparts. But John Hawkes is closer to the French in these matters than any other modern writer I can think of. He has written more criticism than most first-rate American writers do, and he has been readier than most to explain his work seriously in interviews and discussions. In doing this sort of thing, Hawkes has created something like a polemical position for himself. Perhaps because he has done it in this piecemeal and roundabout way, his statements seem unusually free of the self-serving public relations gimmicks that one associates with Robbe-Grillet's frequent position papers. At any rate, I have selected for some serious consideration a statement about his work that Hawkes made in the same interview for *Wisconsin Studies in Contemporary Literature*, from which I quoted his remarks on picaresque above. This statement should help us to see how Hawkes situates his work against the background of previous fiction, and where he would wish us to find the "unique" qualities he mentioned in acknowledging Faulkner's influence on his work.

My novels are not highly plotted, but certainly they're elaborately structured. I began to write fiction on the assumption that the true enemies of the novel were plot, character, setting, and theme, and having once abandoned these familiar ways of thinking about fiction, totality of vision or structure was really all that re-

mained. And structure—verbal and psychological coherence—is
still my largest concern as a writer. Related or corresponding event,
recurring image and recurring action, these constitute the essential
substance or meaningful density of my writing. However, as I
suggested before, this kind of structure can't be planned in advance
but can only be discovered in the writing process itself. The success
of the effort depends on the degree and quality of consciousness
that can be brought to bear on fully liberated materials of the unconscious. I'm trying to hold in balance poetic and novelistic methods in order to make the novel a more valid and pleasurable experience.

This statement tells us a good deal, and there are aspects
of it which I believe we can accept without reservation as
illuminating. There are others about which I feel we should
have some reservations. (I am always suspicious, for instance, of suggestions that fiction can get along without
plot. Both Robbe-Grillet and Hawkes sometimes claim to
have eliminated or suppressed this element in their fiction,
but when I read them I find myself responding to an intense, forward-moving pressure, a real narrative flow. And
this, I say, is what makes their works stories rather than
poems. They may have abandoned certain conventions of
plotting, but I do not think they have abandoned plot.)
But the statement is certainly as good a way into Hawkes's
special world as any other, especially if we understand all its
implications. What I propose to do is examine three parts
of the statement in some detail, working out some of their
implications, in hopes that they will serve to illuminate our
later and more specific consideration of Hawkes's practice
as a fabulator. One is the question of plot vs. structure. A
second is the notion that structure is developed by a process
in which consciousness works on materials liberated from
the unconscious. A third is the notion that this structure

(which can be seen as a balance between poetic and novelistic methods) should lead the reader to a valid and pleasurable experience.

Each of these three parts of the statement points toward a different object. Structure directs our attention to the internal coherence of the works themselves, and beyond that to the art with which they have been put together. The relationship between consciousness and unconsciousness emphasizes both the connection of the works to the psychological processes of the author—along with his understanding of them—and by extension to all mental processes; Hawkes means to use conscious thought and art to illuminate the unconscious, to show us things about ourselves which may be locked in our own unconscious minds, avoiding the scrutiny of our consciousness. Finally, the notions of pleasure and validity point directly to our experience as readers—in two different ways. Hawkes feels that his aim is to produce a "more" valid experience. More valid than what? More valid, I should think, than that of the "conventional" novel, and perhaps more valid than our experience of day-to-day living as well. But why "valid" in particular, rather than "real" or "true"—more common words for the rational content of fiction? The word has interesting implications. "Real" would point to an absolute and empirically verifiable sort of truth—scientific, the truth of "realism." "True" would also suggest an absolute, not physical but metaphysical. "Valid," on the other hand, introduces a less comprehensive kind of accuracy, suggesting an internal coherence rather than a correct statement about something outside the work itself. In logic, a proposition is valid if its conclusion is correctly derived from its premises. But validity, precisely because of its self-checking characteristic, is never relative. It is a logical absolute. No proposition is *more* valid than another. Thus when Hawkes uses the expression "more valid" he is removing the quality of validity from its precise application in logic and employing it in another context. In what sense can a fiction have qualities analogous to logical validity? In the sense of internal consistency, one supposes, but Hawkes seems to be aiming here at a consistency beyond the internal.

He is suggesting that the validity he is aiming for—and the pleasure he hopes to give—are functions of his attempt (a) to balance poetic and novelistic methods, and (b) to apply conscious consideration to materials from the unconscious. Thus "validity," in this context, becomes both a matter of art and of life, of form and of content. It involves discovery and creation simultaneously. The artist, by his method of composition, which is as unplanned as possible, proceeding by recurrences and correspondences rather than logical or chronological sequence, seeks to induce a sort of dreamlike state—first in himself, last in his audience. Durrell's Arnauti, we remember, wanted to set his book "free to dream." Hawkes wants to keep his esthetic superego sufficiently dormant to allow dark materials to well up from his subconscious. Then—when they are "fully liberated"—he will turn the machinery of his consciousness—tuned as delicately as possible—upon these materials. The ideal reader of Hawkes should probably participate in a reciprocal fashion: his delicately tuned consciousness will lead him finally into the ideal dreamlike state; but if he reads with inert incomprehension he will never experience the book at all. As the writer moves from unconscious materials to conscious deployment of them, the reader must move from conscious reception to an awareness of the unconscious.

A notion something like the old surrealistic method of "automatic writing" seems to lie behind Hawkes's formulation here. Except that André Breton and the surrealists would have been horrified at the thought of allowing consciousness to work on these precious materials. Hawkes, on the other hand, insists that a valid structure in fiction depends on the combination of conscious thought with materials from beyond consciousness—just as a successful psychoanalysis depends on the analyst's skill in first helping the patient expose and liberate the sources of his anxieties or neuroses, and then (almost simultaneously) in making a valid interpretation of the symbols through which these materials are manifested. Hawkes has modeled his manner of proceeding as a fabulator, apparently, on the techniques of psychoanalysis. Thus his works are most likely to find their justification in terms of psychic value. Not, like pure romance, in terms of the pleasures of wish-fulfillment; nor, like intellectual comedy, in the joy of perceiving the world as ordered and rationalized by a comic vision; but in terms of the psychic relief of facing our fears and anxieties to grapple with them rather than flee from them.

Now, the last thing I wish to do here is suggest a hierarchy of values for the different modes of fabulation. I believe we need them all—need all our dreams and all our laughter. But at this point I must emphasize our need for the kind of nightmare experience which Hawkes is most concerned with giving us. One need not be a Jungian to see how important it is for man to face his "shadow." Conrad was thinking of this need when he worked out that extraordinary fabulation, "The Heart of Darkness." In Conrad's view, if man does not face and acknowledge the dark in him in order to struggle with it, he will become its victim.

Kurtz is "hollow" because he thinks he has reached a pitch of civilization safely beyond savagery. This is why he is such an easy convert to the bestial. Hawkes, in virtually all of his fabulations, seems in search of ways to liberate images from the heart of darkness so that they may awake in the reader an emotional consciousness of evil along with a shock of recognition.

At this point we have considered—perhaps as extensively as one should without a text in front of him—two of the three aspects of Hawkes's statement. We have yet to consider the distinction between plot and structure. This is a very slippery area in narrative theory, and it will probably be well to set out a few guide-lines before plunging into it. There is a sense, of course, in which we immediately understand the point Hawkes is making about his fiction. He has certainly turned away from orthodox plotting. And he has turned in the opposite direction from a writer like John Barth, who has chosen to emphasize plot more than the realistic novelists did, rather than to reduce its role in his fabulations. But there is a kind of counter-movement in both these turns. By his exaggeration of "plottiness" in a work like *The Sot-Weed Factor,* Barth finally causes us to take his plot more lightly than we might take a less rococo arrangement of events. A sort of esthetic inflation operates, which makes such plotting—as in *Tom Jones*—less serious as it becomes more energetic. A highly plotted novel *wants* to become comic. This has always been an esthetic problem for the writer of romance. Fielding and Barth, in the works mentioned, take advantage of this comic momentum by making the tone and decor of their works enhance this comic plotting.

Similarly, by reducing the overt plottiness of his fiction,

Hawkes generates an intense reaction to such elements of plot as remain there. If Barth gives us the sense of being on a great roller-coaster ride, in which we move up and down—but always safely on a track, Hawkes seems to place us in an emotional quick-sand where we struggle painfully for every inch, and finish with a sense of great achievement when we lie gasping on firm ground a few steps from where we began. Thus by driving his plot underground Hawkes has made it less visible but no less important. His work *is* poetical, in his sense, of course. That is, it is a tissue of recurring and corresponding images and verbal patterns which are emotionally and intellectually meaningful. But his fabulations are not poems; they always depend on some sort of narrative impetus to keep the reader moving. The recurring beads are held together by a string of plot. The buried string of events attracts our attention and draws us toward it, so that we prize it all the more when we have discovered it and experienced it. The dislocations of time and space in Hawkes's work serve the same purpose that they do in Conrad, Ford, and Faulkner. They involve the reader in the constructive process, making him help to create the story.

I have been writing with all of Hawkes's fiction in mind —to the extent that I could hold it there—but this is not a really satisfactory way to proceed. It is time to look at specific works. I have chosen *The Lime Twig* for fairly extended treatment because it seems to me representative of the controlled wit and power which animates Hawkes's mature work. But before turning to it, I wish to pause a moment over an early and somewhat neglected piece: his first long fiction, *Charivari*.

Charivari is militantly *avant-garde*, not in the philosophical sense employed by Hawkes in speaking of a perpetual avant-gardism, but in the more trivial sense of formally shocking. After appearing in a *New Directions* anthology it has remained unprinted—the only one of Hawkes's fabulations not published in book form. It seems at once more aggressive and more tentative than the nearly contemporary *Cannibal*: more certain of what it is not, less certain of what it is; closer to Nathanael West, more overtly surrealistic and psychoanalytical, but less richly and deeply imagined. Perhaps we have in this work an excess of conscious effort working on an insufficiency of materials liberated from the unconscious. It is, then, not a great performance, but it has a special importance for us because it reveals so much about the roots of Hawkes's fiction. It also has the special charm that often accompanies youthful precociousness. I, for one, should like to see it reprinted in a separate volume. But because of its relative inaccessibility, I will assume my readers have not read it.

The book's aggressiveness begins with its title: a word to be looked up. Unlike Hawkes's other titles which are words to be understood in context, this word provides a context for understanding the book.

Charivari. . . . A serenade of "rough music," with kettles, pans, tea-trays, and the like, used in France, in mockery and derision of incongruous or unpopular marriages. . . .   The *OED*.

This particular *Charivari* is a surrealistic examination of the marriage of two "typical" well-to-do modern people. The married couple are a pair of forty-year-old children, faced with the fact that the "bride," after fourteen years of marriage, has become pregnant. The ground plan of the narrative covers two days in the lives of the married couple—two days mainly devoted to a houseparty of West/Fitzgerald and Waugh/Huxley tone and dimensions. In the course of these two days both husband and wife make forays away from their home, where the party is in progress. The husband rides a bus into town, considers picking up a woman who resembles his wife, and is finally brought back home like a runaway child in his father's limousine. The woman drowns in a wild storm. The wife too makes a child-like limousine voyage—accompanied by her mother—to have her pregnancy verified (with overtones of abortion) by a doctor who finds it hysterical (or aborts it) much to everyone's relief. When she returns, miraculously restored to youth by the doctor's discovery, the party continues with fun and games:

> When she ran across the lawn, hair loose and flying, colored skirt whirling about her knees, he knew she was not going to have a child. The flowers around her neck were white with dew, and as she ran she laughed, and her face was momentarily bright.
>
> "My goodness," thought Henry, "she *does* look young." She ran quickly towards him.
>
> Gaylor blew loudly on his whistle. "All right," he called, "it's time to play."

The two excursions from the party are used by Hawkes as ways of illuminating the suppressed fears and desires of Emily and Henry. These two, racked by a fear of growing up, of living as adults and hence of dying, represent aspects of the modern cult of youth. And the entire work, borrowing its hallucinatory technique from surrealism and such originals as the Circe episode of Joyce's *Ulysses*—where hallucination is employed mainly to act out sexual fantasy —can be seen as a bitter satirical fantasy of the Nathanael West variety. It also has a good deal in common with the early Albee play *The American Dream*. Both Hawkes and

Albee, in these early works, seem to have found surrealism a handy vehicle for attacking contemporary mores. Later on, one suspects, they became dissatisfied with using such a powerful weapon on such easy targets. Both the Albee play and *Charivari* are full of delightful exuberance and joy in the mastery of technique—the joy of the fabulator realizing his skills. But their display of skill invites us to question their employment of it. In many writers—one thinks of Jane Austen's parodies or some of Joyce's supercilious epiphanies—the easy satirical victories of youth pave the way for more searching and problematic achievements later on. To realize this, however, is not the same as to wish such works unwritten. In addition to such interest as they have in themselves, they are often of special value as ways into the mind and art of their authors. The cruder values and more blatant displays of the early work may help us to understand the more complex values and more subtle techniques of mature work. *Charivari* is in itself quite good indeed—more interesting than Albee's *American Dream* I should say—and in it we can find some clear examples of the attitudes and techniques which, in more refined form, shape the later works. One of the most important attitudes, one, in fact, which seems to be a governing attitude throughout all of Hawkes's work, is the attitude toward cruelty in fiction which the narrator of *Charivari* formulates with a bold directness and simplicity that we shall not find elsewhere in his fiction:

And have you heard, or do you think we are likely to hear what very private shames and resentments and misgivings these people are harboring? May we be cruel enough?

Something like this purpose seems to animate all of Hawkes's fabulation. The cruelty and brutality of the work

are there in order to expose private shames and resentments. But this statement in *Charivari* is a bit too compla-
cent about locating the shames and resentments in the
characters only—"these people." A sense is established of
reader and narrator conniving to expose "them." In the
later works the exposure involves *us* as well as *them*. Here
the reader's psyche is insulated from emotional complicity
by a curtain of satiric detachment which Hawkes drops
between reader and characters. To me, this sort of detachment is an aspect of the special kind of youthful idealism
one encounters in contemporary student rebellions. The
word at Berkeley during the free-speech demonstrations
was, "Don't trust anyone over thirty." The pathos of this
slogan lies in its acceptance of the connection between this
kind of idealism and immaturity. The old have "sold out."
They have what Hawkes has called here "private shames
and resentments" which inhibit their devotion to the ideal.
The characters of picaresque are usually "them." Rogues
and whores, outcasts and outlaws. But picaresque depends
for its effect on our sense of some common conditions
uniting us and them: common outlandish impulses, perhaps, and a common suspicion of the way things happen—
a sense of the unfitness of things. *Charivari*, however, is less
picaresque in spirit than Hawkes's later work. It is a satire
of manners, really. And Hawkes's growth as a writer has
involved developing beyond satire. His cruel and clever
wit finds its true scope in works like *The Lime Twig* and
Second Skin, where it functions more circumspectly and
humanely.

The view of himself presented by Hawkes in the interview I quoted earlier emphasizes the quality of cold witti-
ness present in his work. It does not direct our attention

to the delicate sensibility which is married to that wit in the later works, and in isolated passages even of *Charivari*. Here, I suspect, we may have a blind spot in the writer's self-scrutiny. He may be unaware of—or reluctant to recognize—the extent to which his work depends not on wit alone, but on wit and tenderness interacting. The source of his narrative power, it seems to me, is located at the point where his cruel wit and delicate sensibility converge to generate the special tonal qualities which mark his best work. I think we have some of his best work in *The Lime Twig*, and I propose to examine some of it here in detail.

III   "THE LIME TWIG"

To trace the interconnections between cruelty and tenderness in *The Lime Twig*, I must try to concentrate closely on the texture of particular passages, but in the context of the work's total structure. To do this I am going to consider a fairly large block of narrative, Chapters 6 and 7 (pp. 123–62 in the New Directions paperback). In dealing closely with so much material, I am necessarily going to assume a reader who has his copy and can follow my references back and forth, but I shall try to quote the really vital passages as well. These chapters do not provide the most dazzling verbal pyrotechnics of the book. There are other passages and episodes more brilliant in themselves—the superb unloading of Rock Castle from the barge, for instance, with the Faulknerian rhythms Hawkes acknowledged (see above, p. 60). But these two chapters will serve quite well to illustrate the way Hawkes qualifies and controls the cruel vision of his later works. They will also provide a narrative unit sizable enough for some consideration of the way plot and structure operate in this work. And finally, since brutality and cruelty are not only matters of the novelist's vision in these chapters but their subject matter as well, this discussion can be the occasion to face the special problem of responding to the brutal in Hawkes's work.

The problem is apparently a real one, since it seems to bother reviewers and ordinary readers alike. It is related to similar responses to quite different writers, however, those writers who can be lumped with Hawkes as Black Humorists. For certain readers and reviewers Black Humor is apparently a synonym for "offensive"; thus it can be applied indiscriminately to the excremental gaiety of Barth's *Sot-Weed Factor*, the jolly stoicism of Vonnegut's *Cat's Cradle*, or the chilling cruelty of *The Lime Twig*. Against such blanket indictments there can be no rational defense, but there is a more serious and pointed charge which is sometimes made specifically against Hawkes. This is worth some attention. A convenient statement of this charge happened (as it was meant to, no doubt) to arrive in my mail box recently in the form of a review of Hawkes's last novel, *Second Skin*. The editor-in-chief of a new quarterly review, *Salmagundi*, charges Hawkes with playing "to the expectation of an audience which is if anything too ready to embrace violence and madness as a norm, at least insofar as 'artistic' reflections of experience are concerned." And he adds the following two strictures, which seem fairly to sum up a whole line of argument against the kind of thing Hawkes is doing:

> The appallingly violent character of the experience depicted in *Second Skin*, while it washes over our sensorium, is not something to which we can intellectually attest. It is not a truth I can affirm

from the experience I know, and is therefore not creditable as a viable representation of our common situation. . . .

That a John Hawkes should feel compelled to dwell on morbidity and perversion because it is expected of him, because to do so is somehow part of his function, is indeed lamentable.

These criticisms, though directed at *Second Skin*, could apply equally well to *The Lime Twig*, which is just as well stocked with materials this reviewer would call appallingly violent, morbid, and perverse. As I understand this line of attack it makes two related charges against Hawkes: (a) that his work is not a valid record of common experience, and (b) that it is morbid, indulging in excesses of brutality when it could be persuading us to some sort of uplifting social commitment. The first point can be disposed of briefly. Extremes of violence such as those given us in Chapter 6 of *The Lime Twig* are not common experiences, but they are frequent enough for such scenes in fiction to have innumerable counterparts in journalism. In war and in peace, man is often a brutal animal. Furthermore, even those who have never been personally involved in external violence (surely not a large majority in these militant decades) must find in their responses to fictional cruelty and brutality genuine psychic echoes of these fictional events. The second point is both harder and easier to answer. As for the writer's responsibility to make the world better rather than worse, I certainly acknowledge it. But the writer of fiction is concerned with his reader as an individual. His aim is to exercise the separate sensibilities of his readership, not to weld them into a great society. But even if this is so, point (b) is not fully answered until we have considered the uses of what the reviewer calls "morbidity and perversion." To deal with this question fairly, we must have a text in front of us. Chapter 6 of *The Lime Twig* ought to be a fair test.

The central event of this chapter is the beating of innocent Margaret Banks by the brutal mobster Thick. Margaret's attempt to escape has given this sadist an excuse to go to work on her with his rubber truncheon:

His arm went up quivering, over his head with the truncheon falling back, and came down hard and solid as a length of cold fat stripped from a pig, and the truncheon beat into her just above the knee; then into the flesh of her mid-thigh; then on her hips; and on the tops of her legs. And each blow quicker and harder than the last, until the strokes went wild and he was aiming randomly at abdomen and loins, the thin fat and the flesh that was deeper, each time letting the rubber lie where it landed then drawing the length of it across stomach or pit of stomach or hip before raising it to the air once more and swinging it down. It made a sound like a dead bird falling to empty field. Once he stopped to increase the volume of the radio, but returned to the bedside, shuffling, squinting down at her, his mouth a separate organ paralyzed in the lower part of his face, and paused deceptively and then made a rapid swing at her, a feint and then the loudest blow of all so swiftly that she could not gasp. When he finally stopped for good she was bleeding, but not from any wound she could see.

We know why Thick does this; the question is why does Hawkes feel obliged to devote a chapter to it, why does he present it so elaborately, why, in fact, does he present it at all? Is this a perverse indulgence, a wallowing in brutality for its own sake?

These questions should be considered from two aspects. One has to do with the function of this chapter in the narrative as a whole: the degree to which it can be accounted for in terms of specific contributions to the larger scheme. The other has to do with the way brutality and cruelty are presented here; in comparison with other works which present us with the cruel and brutal, to what extent does this work seem wantonly sadistic? The second question, if answered satisfactorily, should help us to answer the first. The more clearly we see what is going on when Thick beats Margaret, the better we will be able to understand the relationship of this scene to the rest of the book.

First of all, we need to remind ourselves that there are beatings and beatings—many ways of actually hurting people and many ways of describing or representing any such occurrence in literature. An examination of some scenes from other works of fiction may help us to put this one in perspective. First of all, consider this familiar episode:

Stephen closed his eyes and held out in the air his trembling hand with the palm upwards. He felt the prefect of studies touch it for a moment at the fingers to straighten it and then the swish of the sleeve of the soutane as the pandybat was lifted to strike. A hot burning stinging tingling blow like the loud crack of a broken stick made his trembling hand crumple together like a leaf in the fire: and at the sound and the pain scalding tears were driven into his eyes. His whole body was shaking with fright, his arm was shaking and his crumpled burning livid hand shook like a loose leaf in the air. A cry sprang to his lips, a prayer to be let off. But though the tears scalded his eyes and his limbs quivered with pain and fright he held back the hot tears and the cry that scalded his throat.

This beating is not finished. There is another hand to come. But we have enough to see what Joyce is up to. His main effort is to render the physical pain undergone by Stephen and the associated emotional pain: the "hot burning stinging tingling blow," the "fierce maddening stinging tingling pain," followed by "a palsy of fright" and the "scalding cry" and "scalding tears" which well up in

Stephen to his "shame" and "rage." Joyce's rendering of physical pain here should help us see how little Hawkes is concerned to render it: in fact, how carefully he avoids it. It is not Margaret's pain but her situation as helpless victim which Hawkes is rendering. Joyce's simile of Stephen's hand crumpling like "a leaf in the fire" is just one detail in a whole sequence of high-temperature imagery Joyce uses as the most potent means of evoking pain. (Hell is fiery for the same reason.) Hawkes, however, emphasizes the coldness of the weapon and its ugly sexuality ("hard and solid as a length of cold fat stripped from a pig") and in his most elaborate image compares the sound of the blows to "a dead bird falling to empty field." This image is telling us more about Margaret's situation as lonely victim than about the sound it is ostensibly aimed at rendering. Sympathetic fear, not empathetic pain, is the emotional effect actually sought by the prose in this passage.

For another perspective on cruelty, consider this passage from a less familiar work:

> The air immediately resounds to the whistle of lashes and the thud of stripes sinking into lovely flesh; Octavie's screams mingle with the sounds of leather, the monk's curses reply: what a scene for these libertines surrendering themselves to a thousand obscenities in the midst of us all! They applaud him, they cheer him on; however, Octavie's skin changes color, the brightest tints incarnadine join the lily sparkle; but what might perhaps divert Love for an instant, were moderation to have direction of the sacrifice, becomes, thanks to severity, a frightful crime against Love's laws; nothing stops or slows the perfidious monk, the more the young student complains, the more the professor's harshness explodes; from the back to the knee, everything is treated in the same way, and it is at last upon his barbaric pleasures' blood-drenched vestiges the savage quenches his flames.

This is the real thing, Sadism with a capital S, from *Justine*. The obvious parallels with the scene in *The Lime Twig* should be noted: the innocent female victim, the brute who takes pleasure in her pain, the viciousness of the beating itself. But the differences in the two scenes far outweigh their surface similarities. In Sade, the effects of the beating are themselves described in voluptuous terms: "the brightest tints incarnadine join the lily sparkle"; and the subject, though finally beaten to a pulp, is afterward a fit subject for further abuses:

> The rest of the *soirée* would have resembled all the others had it not been for the beauty and the touching age of this young maiden who more than usually inflamed those villains and caused them to multiply their infamies; it was satiety rather than commiseration that sent the unhappy child back to her room and gave her, for a few hours at least, the rest and quiet she needed.

This orgy makes an hour with Thick and his truncheon seem like a pleasant massage in comparison—yet no permanent damage is done. De Sade's characters are inexhaustible and indestructible. They are exactly skin deep. His fantasies are truly erotic because he separates pain from destruction, making it a mere sensation rather than an expression of bodily malaise. We do not sympathize with the objects of de Sade's voluptuous fantasies because they are so indestructible, like some special kind of doll which not only wets its panties and says mamma but bleeds when whipped—all without in any way suggesting actual human life. But Margaret Banks is hurt by her beating—not just pained but damaged, physically and psychologically:

> Thick had been too rough with her, treated her too roughly, and some things didn't tolerate surviving, some parts of her couldn't

stand a beating. She hadn't even her free hands with which to rub
them. (p. 130)

. . . a wetness under the eye exposed to the wash of light and the
sobs just bubbling on the lips. Margaret inert, immobile, young
woman with insides ruptured and fingers curling at the moment of
giving sound to her grievance. (p. 131)

We are a long way from de Sade here. But we are not
with the sentimentalists, indulging in a "good cry" over a
poor victim. Hawkes has worked in a number of ways to
frustrate any attempt we make to descend into mere senti-
mentality here. He is, as in all his best work, trying to construct what Rilke called a "bridge barely curved that connects the terrible with the tender." And even in this scene,
the bridge of his sympathetic perception is braced and
stiffened by his cold and grotesque wit. Margaret's relief
(p. 128) at the thought that Thick has his truncheon and
will not be reduced to his favorite substitute is—even under the circumstances—comic: "she thought that a wet
newspaper would be unbearable." The pitiful inadequacy
of this response to her situation, which is unbearable in any
case, is pathetic. But Margaret's maintenance of her own
prim perspective under these terrible circumstances, the
incongruous rigidity of her mental processes, qualifies the
pathos of her situation. Her perception of Thick as a sort
of naughty child also has in it a bizarre mixture of appropriateness and incongruity. His truncheon makes "her think
of a bean bag, an amusement for a child," which is partly
just an inadequate response to the threat in the instrument,
derived from Margaret's innocence, and partly a very
shrewd perception of Thick's childishness. This sort of
complication, which prevents any easy sentimental response
to these brutal events, is also in evidence in the complicity

of understanding (as between mother and naughty child) between her and Thick. The paragraph just preceding the actual beating is an extraordinary one:

Then something happened to his face. To the mouth, really. The sour sweat was there and the mouth went white, so rigid and distended that for a moment he couldn't speak: yet all at once she knew, knew well enough the kinds of things he was saying—to himself, to her—and in the darkness and hearing the faint symphonic program, she was suddenly surprised that he could say such things.

Innocent Margaret is surprised that Thick can think the things she attributes to him. He does not speak aloud, but she understands whatever sadistic ravings are implied by that white, rigid, distended mouth. And so do we. She is surprised that Thick "could say such things." We are surprised that Margaret can find words for thoughts that so surprise her. But we know what she means he means. By her understanding she becomes a kind of accomplice to this crime of sadism. And by ours we share that guilt.

A further dimension, also partly comic, is added to these events by the matter-of-factness Margaret maintains throughout. A touch of pride enters into the way she conceives of her experience. She is "like a convent girl accepting the mysteries . . . and no matter how much she accepted she knew it now: something they couldn't show in films." To conceive the inconceivable elements of her experience she tries to frame it in religious or cinematic terms. It is like an initiation into inconceivable "mysteries," and it is too outlandish to be put on the screen. These terms, again both pitifully inadequate and curiously appropriate, make Margaret's situation both poignantly accessible to us and ironically distanced from our own situations. Thus Hawkes, by intertwining comic and pathetic elements, has generated a situation so fraught with tones and attitudes that no simple emotional reaction is adequate to it. And when we consider the relationship between the events of this chapter and the rest of the story, we find further important lines of connection sufficient to dispel any notion we might still have that the brutality we have been considering is gratuitous or indulged in for its own sake.

Margaret's destruction, of course, is "undeserved." In the picaresque world this is the way things happen; rewards and punishments are incongruous and inappropriate. But this is not a purely picaresque world. Things happen in a curiously dislocated way, but there is also a kind of logic at work, a kind of plotting behind the apparently random sequence of events which makes the events more meaningful than they could be in a merely episodic structure. In the chapter we have been considering, Margaret suffers because of Michael's involvement with the people who make her suffer. Not only does she become hostage and victim so that the gang will have maximum control over Michael, but, specifically, some of what she suffers has been directly and immediately caused by Michael's actions of the same night—actions which are presented to us *after* we see their results so that we apprehend them colored by their consequences. We are forced to see them ethically.

In Chapter 7, Hawkes chronicles Michael's activities of the same night we have been considering in Chapter 6, and in his presentation he takes care to give us a number of ways to synchronize the two chapters and understand their interrelationship. Actually, Chapter 7 overlaps Chapter 6 chronologically. Chapter 6 begins at "4 A.M.," after Margaret's partial recovery from Thick's violence (which is narrated in a flash-back). The chapter ends with Larry's additional violence. He slashes Margaret's wrists as he cuts the ropes that have tied her to the bed:

> "You've wounded me," she whispered, eyes to the ceiling and in darkness. "You cut me."
> He said only: "I meant to cut you, Miss. . . ."
> So sometime after 4 A.M. she tried to use her numb and sleeping arms, twice struck out at him, then found her hands, the bleeding wrists, the elbows, and at last her cheek going down beneath and against the solid sheen of his bullet-proof vest.

This rape of Margaret is the final violence of the sixth chapter. And among our other reactions it leaves us wondering whether there might have been any particular reason for Larry's cruelty here; we wonder why he "meant" to cut Margaret. The next chapter provides our answer, but not at first. It begins earlier, at "2 A.M. of the last night he spent alive," with Michael cavorting in bed with Larry's girl Sybilline. Her task has been to keep Michael docile and amused until the race is over, but she has apparently exceeded the call of duty, having "given a single promise and three times already made it good." And this is only the beginning of a night of surrealistic sexual activity for Michael. Before the evening is over he also contents the widowed landlady; Annie, the girl next door; and finally even Dora. After Annie, he returns to the parlor while Dora and the others are stripping Larry down to his bullet-proof vest:

> The pearl buttons came off the shirt and Banks stepped no closer, though Sybilline was there and laughing on one of Larry's arms. "Oh, do what Little Dora says," he heard her cry, "I want

you to!" And there was a bruise, a fresh nasty bruise, beneath Syb's eye. (p. 158)

The bruise is the first part of Larry's reaction to Sybilline's behavior with Michael. The rape of Margaret is the final part: "he was cock of this house." Thus after Michael retires to engage in his final sexual activity of the evening —this time with Dora—Larry, with his torso bare except for the bullet-proof vest, visits Margaret. By giving us the timing of the two chapters so precisely—one beginning at four, the other at two—Hawkes helps us to make the necessary synchronization. But he also uses another device, which reaches out beyond synchronization for the book's larger implications. In each chapter we have a bird on a branch. In Chapter 6 Margaret hears it just before Larry enters:

> Outside on a branch above the garbage receptacle, an oven tit was stirring: not singing but moving testily amidst the disorder of leaf, straw sprig, remnant of gorse, fluttering now and then or scratching, making no attempt to disguise the mood, the pallidness, which later it would affect to conceal in liveliness and muted song. A warbler. But a sleepless bird and irritable. Through drowsiness and barge-heavy pain she noticed the sounds of it and did not smile; saw rather a panorama of chimneys, fine rain, officers of the law and low yards empty of children; farther off there was a heap of tile and a young woman in rubber shoes, an apron and wide white cap, and there were bloodstains on the ticking.

In Chapter 7 Michael hears its mate:

> The mate of the oven tit had found a branch outside his window and he heard its damp scratching and its talk. Even two oven tits may be snared and separated in such a dawn. He listened, turned his head under the shadows, and reflected that the little bird was fagged. And he could feel the wet light rising round all the broken doors, the slatted crevices, rising round the fens, the dripping petrol pump, up the calves and thighs of the public and deserted visions

of the naked man—the fire put out in the steam-bath alley, the kitchen fire drowned, himself fagged and tasteless as the bird on the sick bough.

The birds serve to link the two chapters and the two characters. This evening with its bizarre and strenuous activities has seen them both receive initiation "into the mysteries." In their separate beds they have explored the world of violence and sensuality. Margaret's excess of pain and suffering has been ironically balanced by Michael's excess of "pleasure." But they are both doomed. It is the last night for both. They are like birds lured to a lime twig and stuck fast for destruction. The two chapters end almost simultaneously. Little Monica discreetly runs out of Margaret's room as Larry begins his assault, only to be shot by the absurd constable. Michael, pricked by one of the pearls Sybilline lost in his bed, fingers it idly and drops it ("lost the pearl for good") just as the constable's shot explodes in his ears.

Michael has become like one of those characters in folk literature (often doomed), who have their wishes granted. Annie's appearance at the orgy is simply the result of Michael's having lusted after her—the girl next door—at one time or another. The whole involvement of Michael and Margaret with Larry and the gang is the result of another wish fulfilled—a dream: "his own worst dream, and best, was of a horse which was itself the flesh of all violent dreams." Hencher is the fairy godmother who grants Michael his wish. The destruction that ensues has been lurking in Michael's dream all along. "If wishes were horses, beggars would ride," our folk wisdom tells us. And when Michael's wish takes on the form of horseflesh, Michael rides out to his destruction. He "rides" sexually throughout that long pre-race orgy. And he races out across the track on the day of the Golden Bowl to throw himself in the path of the destructive energy he has unleashed, to bring to a halt the terrible motion of his dream fulfilled. This act of self-destruction redeems Michael, returns him from the brutal dream world of Larry and Syb to the ordinary world of humanity. He atones for the crimes he has helped set in motion, and especially for what his dream has done to Margaret—that suffering of which we readers are so well aware. At the moment of Michael's death a voice—it must be half-dead Margaret's—asks "take me out to him, please," ratifying with this loyalty and care Michael's decision to break the hold of the dream upon him by meeting it head-on.

In *The Lime Twig* Hawkes has gone well beyond the easy satire of *Charivari* to a richer, more complex mode of narrative. By pruning somewhat his surrealistic exuberance, and coming to terms (even if somewhat ironic and parodic ones) with fiction's need for plot, he has achieved a controlled intensity of effect which bridges beautifully the gap between terror and tenderness. This effect is based partly on the balance he maintains between the delicately serious and the grotesquely comic, and partly on the way he has ordered the flow of information about the events of the story as they enter our consciousness. He demands a resolutely alert reader, willing to pay close attention to detail and piece out from dislocated hints the real fabric of events: what has happened, what is happening, and what is going to happen.

In the two chapters which I have been discussing, the order in which the fictional events enter our consciousness has much to do with our attitude toward them and toward the whole narrative. We know why Thick beats Margaret, but we have to wonder about why Larry cuts her, finally reaching understanding through an inference based on the fresh bruise under Sybilline's eye. Our discoveries about the timing of events also serve to enrich our attitude toward them. At 4 A.M. Margaret is recovering from the beating she received "several hours" earlier. At 2 A.M. Michael has finished his third "commotion" with Sybilline. So we must conclude that Thick's sadistic performance and Michael's more normally erotic one were cruelly synchronous.

In *The Lime Twig* the very language in which events are described conspires to suggest connections and correlations with other events. Thick's truncheon, sounding like "a dead bird falling to empty field," is subtly and ironically connected to Michael's flinging aside the widow's whalebone stay "as he might a branch in a tangled wood." Birds and branches are woven all through *The Lime Twig*, making a tapestry of images which elaborates on the motif of the title. Michael is ominously greeted by a "tiny black bird" (p. 30) as he stands near his and Margaret's bed at the beginning of the day in which he becomes involved in "this crime." Lying in bed and plotting, Hencher hears "a little bird trying to sing on the ledge where the Kidneys used to freeze" (p. 28). This interweaving of images around the title motif (which one could follow at much greater length than I have here) must be the sort of thing Hawkes had in mind when he spoke of introducing a poetic structure into his work in place of the traditional plot. But this structure in *The Lime Twig* is subordinated to the more peculiarly narrative structure of multiple suspense which gives the story its driving force.

One of the things I am trying to suggest here is that this

kind of book, which seems so foggy and dreamlike, is actually as neatly and tightly put together as the electrical circuitry of the human nervous system. In his perceptive introduction to the book, Leslie Fiedler makes one emphasis which I should like to reverse. He suggests that Hawkes "does not abandon all form in his quest for the illusion of formlessness." I should like to go much further, to say that not only are there what Fiedler calls "occasions for wit and grace" in the book, but that it has been plotted with a grace and constructed with a wit that makes the whole story not a "random conjunction" but a true fabulation—a more satisfying piece of work than any casual construct, no matter how full of occasional graces, might be. The revulsion inherent in facing the shadow of terror is turned into a pleasurable experience for Hawkes's readers precisely by means of his care for form. It is the form —and the sense it gives us of connections and correspondences, along with the feeling of controlled movement from tension to stability—which makes such terrible materials not merely bearable but beautiful. This is what makes Hawkes a fabulator like the one described in the fable: capable of rejoicing us when we are heavy. The joy that goes into the fabulation is returned to us in the reading. And it is for this joy that we must be grateful, even to the darkest of fabulators.

CHAPTER 5 FABULATION AND ALLEGORY

I ALLEGORY

Once there was a country called Fiction, bordered on one
side by the mountains of Philosophy and on the other by
a great bog called History. The people of Fiction had a
great gift, the gift of telling stories which could amuse men.
As long as they had no contact with the peoples of the
neighboring territories they were perfectly satisfied with
their gift and wanted nothing. But progress, and improved
communications, brought them into contact with the
strange peoples who lived on their borders and beyond.
These peoples were not story-tellers like the Fiction people,
but they had something called Ideas. And when the Fiction people learned about Ideas they yearned for them
terribly and wanted to use them to give their stories more
dignity. A story without Ideas, they came to think, was
fit only for children. So the Fiction people agreed that they
would begin trading with their neighbors to get some Ideas.

97

This only made things worse. For the people on the Philosophy side of the land of Fiction insisted that Fictional Ideas should come from Philosophy, or from Theology just back in the hills, while the people on the other side said the only Ideas any good for fiction were those of the Historians. For a while those who favored Philosophy and Theology won. They called their part of Fiction "Allegory" and they flourished under leaders like Dante and Spenser. But after a while the Ideas from Philosophy and Theology began to lose their zip, and even the Philosophers started saying that the Historians had a lot of good Ideas. Then the Allegorists grew weak and the other party, who called themselves "Realists," began to grow in size and power. They took Ideas from the Historians and discovered other territories, way back in the bog, peopled by an aggressive breed known as Social Scientists. These fellows had Ideas too, and the Realists took as many as they could get.

Then a strange thing happened. The Historians and Social Scientists got tired of having other folks put their Ideas into stories. They decided to muscle in on the story racket themselves. So they climbed out of the bog and invaded the fertile fields of Fiction, and everybody who stayed on in the territory they occupied had to agree to write non-Fiction novels. At the same time the Philosophers and Theologians got a whole new batch of Ideas called Existentialism and Wittgenstein which frightened them so much that they lit out for the highest peaks leaving Ideas strewn all over the foothills. But some Philosophers had got to like that territory so much that they wouldn't leave. They were still there when the refugees from Realism started to pour in and take over. Finally, in order to stay, they had to agree to show these refugees a new way to do Allegory with all these new Ideas. A few of the refugees had smuggled some Ideas called Jung and Freud with them, and when the leftover Philosophers saw them they said they weren't Social Science Ideas anyway, but things those rascals had stolen from Theology and Philosophy to begin with. So they took all the old and new Ideas they could find and began trying to work out a new kind of Allegory. One of the leftover Philosophers who showed the refugees from Fiction the most was a nice lady named Iris Murdoch.

Well. This little exemplum is a pretty feeble fable, just a discursive convenience, really, and not a proper allegory. Its characters and events are too shadowy, of too little interest in themselves, to be thought of as truly allegorical. In the great allegories, tension between the ideas illustrated by the characters and the human qualities in their characterization makes for a much richer and more powerful kind of meaning. The great allegories are never entirely allegorical, just as the great realistic novels are never entirely real. And, in allegory, it is often the tension between the ideational side of a situation and the human side which makes for the power and the meaning—and the power *of* the meaning. Take, for example, the concept of damnation, which is derived from analogies with actual punishment by torture but is referred to an "ideal" eternal world outside the visible universe. And take also a little human situation, a pair of young lovers such as might people a harmless novella of cuckoldry. Put these two things together and you have Francesca da Rimini and her lover Paolo, burning forever in Dante's hell. This is allegory. My fable, on the other hand, was only a nod from criticism in the direction of allegory.

That fable, however, was the shortest and clearest way that I could sketch out my view of the relations of allegory and realism to fiction—both the conceptual relations and the historical ones. Now I must gloss that brief paradigm a bit. Allegory amounts to seeing life through ideational filters provided by philosophy or theology. When realism supplanted allegory as the great form of serious narrative, it claimed to be superior because it looked directly at life —without filters of any kind. The manifestoes of realism are full of terms like "objectivity," "detachment," "experiment," and so on, which suggest a clear and scientific view of life. But we can see now that it is impossible to look directly at life. It is like gazing right into the sun; we see so much that we are blinded.

For a writer, language itself is a great filter, which colors his view of life. For the realistic novelist, other filters in the form of concepts of time, space, causality, society, and a whole collection of psychological types and tropes enable him to capture what he calls "life" on paper. He may be unaware of these, simply imitating his predecessors or seeing in the same way his contemporaries see, but the filters are there—and indispensable—whether the novelist knows it or not. As one of realism's great apologists, Georg Lukács, has put it, realism depends on types:

The central category and criterion of realist literature is the type, a peculiar synthesis which organically binds together the general and the particular both in characters and situations. What makes a type a type is not its average quality, not its mere individual being, however profoundly conceived: what makes it a type is that in it all the humanly and socially essential determinants are present on their highest level of development, in the ultimate unfolding of the possibilities latent in them, in extreme presentation of their extremes, rendering concrete the peaks and limits of men and epochs.

Allegory also depends on types, but the types of allegory are referable to a philosophy and theology concerned with ideals and essences; while the types of realism are referable to social sciences concerned with recording and understanding the processes that govern existence. The types of realism are committed to the visible world while the types of allegory are committed to the invisible. This is why allegory was the great narrative form of the later Middle Ages and early Renaissance. When the Christian cosmos, based on the invisible world of eternity, was challenged by a humanism that put man and his visible world at the cosmic center of things, allegory became the best literary mode for controlling and reconciling these two visions. Francesca da Rimini in Dante's hell is a perfect example of the invisible world controlling the visible, of Christianity acknowledging humanism but mastering it—with difficulty, of course. That is why Dante faints after hearing Francesca. And the faint of the character Dante reflects the effort expended by the author Dante in giving humanism such a fair display and still keeping it subordinate. In a way, the rise of the novel simply reflects the triumph of humanism and the empirical attitudes which came in its train. As the invisible world lost its reality, the visible world became realer. And as dogmatic theology and systematic philosophy lost their control over men's minds, they were supplanted by positivistic or pragmatic and relativistic views of life and conduct. The realistic novel, which presents views of life and conduct in terms of manners and mores, was the appropriate form for serious fiction in the age of Comte.

But that age is ending. Now positivism, pragmatism, and realism itself are fading and losing their hold on the minds of men. Instead of being The Way, they now just seem a way. They seem like dogma, and tired old dogma at that. Furthermore, psychology, when it moves away from statistics and experiments with animals and probes into the depths of the human psyche, is moving from social science toward philosophy; for the deeps of the psyche are an invisible world also, one which modern men accept with the same unquestioning faith once reserved for the invisible world of Christianity. Freud and Jung together have presented the modern writer with a new scheme of the invisible world which cries out for allegorization. The depths, of course, are murkier than the heavens, and any allegory based on depth psychology will have to be more tentative than an allegory based on the Christian cosmos needed to be. But the archetypal system of Joyce's *Finnegans Wake* is as allegorical as anything in Dante.

Joyce's journey from epiphany to archetype is, like Iris Murdoch's move from philosophy to fiction, a sign of the times. Joyce inherited the notion of epiphany from a romantic/symbolist esthetic of the late nineteenth century. As he worked it out and explained it to himself in the too familiar passages of *Stephen Hero,* an epiphany was the way the world revealed itself and its meaning. At certain times or in certain situations, mundane things and people would reveal their essence to the sensitive observer. The observer, detached and objective, needed only to record what he saw to capture the meaning of an aspect of life.

The artist as sensitive observer and recorder of man in nature is a romantic poet. As sensitive observer and recorder of man in society, he is a realistic novelist. As sensitive observer and recorder of the motions of his own soul, he is the romantic/realistic autobiographer—a Rousseau. In Joyce a conception of himself based on this romantic/

realistic notion of the artist's role in life warred with an older notion of the artist as maker and shaper, organizing the raw material of life so as to display the idea of it already in the creator's mind. Joyce's progress, from the early epiphanies and *Chamber Music* through *Dubliners* and *Stephen Hero, A Portrait, Exiles,* and *Ulysses,* to *Finnegans Wake* is a journey from epiphany to archetype; hence, from symbolism to allegory. This journey was made possible by Joyce's discovery of cyclical theories of history (essentially medieval rather than modern because they are based on a notion of control of events in the visible world by an ideal order outside these events), and his parallel discovery of depth psychology—which modernized this medieval view of history by locating the ideal patterns that control the cycles of human life not in the heavens but in the unconscious. The collective unconscious effectively dehumanizes man by de-individualizing him. The social types of Lukács belong to realism. But the archetypes of Jung lead to a new allegory. Jung himself denied this, insisting that "an allegory is a paraphrase of a conscious content, whereas a symbol is the best possible expression for an unconscious content whose nature can only be guessed because still unknown." But once Jung had charted the unconscious and named its symbols, they became available for allegorical use. And this is how Joyce used them.

Finnegans Wake can also serve as the mighty exemplar of another aspect of modern allegorizing. Along with depth psychology, language theory has developed recently as an important new pseudo-science. I tried to suggest these developments in the little exemplum at the beginning of this chapter, but they too must be glossed a bit here. The modern development of semantics, of structural linguistics, and of the philosophy of language in general, has had an immense impact on literature. For one thing, it has led philosophy to serious questioning of its linguistic medium, resulting in both the invention of specially pure languages (symbolic logic) for philosophical thought, and a new concentration on language itself as the best mirror of the human mind.

In *Finnegans Wake* Joyce is partly allegorizing along archetypal lines, using recurrent patterns of birth, fall, death, rebirth, and so on to organize material drawn from throughout history and pre-history. But he is also playing a great language game, embracing the duplicity and ambiguity of his verbal medium, spinning multiplicities of meaning out of puns and portmanteau words. Just a few sentences taken from a passage which focuses on the alphabet and language (*FW*, I.i.) will illustrate how Joyce's two kinds of allegorizing work together in that book:

(Stoop) if you are abcedminded, to this claybook, what curios of signs (please stoop), in this allaphbed! Can you rede (since We and Thou had it out already) its world? It is the same told of all. Many. Miscegenations on miscegenations. Tieckle. They lived and laughed ant loved end left. Forsin. Thy thingdome is given to the Meades and Porsons. The meandertale, aloss and again, of our old Heidenburgh in the days when Head-in-Clouds walked the earth. In the ignorance that implies impression that knits knowledge that finds the nameform that whets the wits that convey contacts that sweeten sensation that drives desire that adheres to attachment that dogs death that bitches birth that entails the ensuance of existentiality.

The passage insists that world and word are the same: "Can you rede . . . its world?" It also insists on cyclical historical process, and it merges history as process with his-

tory as recorded and narrated: "It is the same told of all."
Life is a "meandertale" and all its possibilities are contained in its beginning—or in the alphabet—"in this allaphbed." Earth and language make one great "claybook" in
which man's journey from ignorance through knowledge
and desire to procreation and death is written. In the beginning was the word with a vengeance. Joyce's book certainly is for the "abcedminded." The passage, in fact,
would support a good deal more glossification, but I do
not want to dwell on it any longer. *Finnegans Wake* is
splendidly illustrative of the allegorizing trend of modern
fiction. Illustrative but not typical. It is too extreme a case.
Nor would I call it exactly a fabulation. It has the playful
spirit and delight in language, but it lacks the purely narrative value that characterizes fabulation; that delight in
story for its own sake which is so marked in Durrell's *Alexandria Quartet* is lacking in *Finnegans Wake*. Mind you,
this is a matter of classification only, not of evaluation. But
fabulation is my subject, not the whole range of modern
fiction. Joyce is a great allegorist—well christened "Dublin's Dante" by Oliver Gogarty. But neither Dublin's nor
Florence's Dante cared much for mere story. They are
allegorists but not fabulators. Edmund Spenser and Iris
Murdoch are fabulators as well as allegorists. And fabulation always poses special problems. People will come along
who suggest that it should be read for the story only. It
can be read in this way, as I suppose Shakespeare can be
read for the "beauty of his language." But this is hardly
the best way to read them. For in the work of an allegorical fabulator, fiction and ideation are always intertwined.
They do not merely depend on one another; they inter-
penetrate one another. Part of the meaning is *in* the fiction,

of course. But so, also, is part of the fiction *in* the meaning. When something happens to a character who is allegorically conceived, the event takes place simultaneously on the level of fiction and the level of ideation. To show how this process works, and to present for serious consideration one of the fine achievements of modern allegorical fabulation, I have chosen to discuss Iris Murdoch's "Gothic" romance, *The Unicorn*.

II   IRIS MURDOCH'S "UNICORN"

In *The Unicorn* Iris Murdoch is a "Gothic" writer as Isak Dinesen is in *Seven Gothic Tales*. Recently Robert Langbaum, in his exciting study of Dinesen (*The Gaiety of Vision*), has shown us that Dinesen's artificial tales are carefully worked-out romances of ideas—what I would call allegories. The bizarre and artificial elements of her tales are parts of a structure of ideas. This much, I should say, is also true of *The Unicorn*. But, if we can think of these two brilliant ladies as allegorists, Iris Murdoch is "modern" in a way that Isak Dinesen is not. For Isak Dinesen, if Langbaum is right, accepted the romantic view of nature as, in Coleridge's phrase, "the art of God." But modern fabulators are post-realistic and post-romantic as well. They lack that Coleridgean belief in the ultimate order of the world. As John Barth put it: "If you are a novelist of a certain type of temperament, then what you really want to do is re-invent the world. God wasn't too bad a novelist, except he was a Realist." For the post-World War II fabulators, any order they impose on the world amounts not to a symbol of the divine order that God imposed on the cosmos, but to an allegory of the mind of man with its rage for an order superior to that of nature. It amounts to thumbing their noses at You Know Who. Isak Dinesen seems to have been a genuine romantic esthete, whose work implied a God Who was an artist much like herself. Oscar Wilde was an artist stricken with our kind of modernism when he waspishly observed that Wordsworth "found in stones the sermons he had already hidden there." For the writers of today, nature has been both disenchanted and dehumanized. It is merely alien, other. Their choice is simply whether to try and capture this dehumanization in their art—to be "realistic" as *Nausea*, *The Stranger*, and *Jealousy* are—or to hold up to nature an image not of nature itself but of a human order—as Barth and Iris Murdoch do.

The contemporary allegorist is likely to be both arbitrary and tentative. His world will be idealized but unsystematic, full of meanings but devoid of meaning. The world of *The Unicorn* is this kind of world. The world of *Seven Gothic Tales*, which includes such perfect allegories as "The Roads Round Pisa" and "The Poet," is no longer available to the serious fabulator. Isak Dinesen was presenting an esthetic answer to the attack on art made by her compatriot Sören Kierkegaard. Iris Murdoch is a critic and interpreter of Jean-Paul Sartre.

Since every scene, every character, and every event in *The Unicorn* contributes to the plot or the meaning—usually to both simultaneously—we must have a firm grip on the structure of character and events in order to deal with the allegorical dimensions of the tale. As I understand the reading process, we read any story by engaging in what Poe called ratiocination. As we start to read we build up expectations in the form of cloudy and tentative structures, into which we try to fit the details of character and event as they are presented to us. We modify these tentative structures as we are forced to by elements that do not fit, and we seek to perfect them as we move toward the end of the story.

In a work with as much story in it as there is in *The Unicorn* we are given considerable exercise in ratiocination merely in keeping up with events. Take, for example, the opening lines of the book, which begins this way:

"How far away is it?"

That is the first paragraph. It is ostensibly a single question, but it sets up in our structure of expectations at least eight additional questions: 1) What is *it*?; 2) Who wants to know?; 3) Why does he want to know?; 4) Who is he asking?; 5) Does he plan to go to "it"?; 6) Will he get there?; 7) How?; 8) What will he find there? Some of these questions are more important than others, but the reader is not in a position to know which. Some will make themselves felt more consciously than others for different readers. The number of such questions which the reader senses in some way is an indication of the intensity of his response, a measure of his ratiocinative commitment. Some of the eight questions I have listed as probable responses to the opening line actually depend on certain answers to others. Numbers 7 and 8 anticipate a "yes" answer to number 6. The ideal reader, in his structure-building, is probably much like a good chess player, who is always thinking ahead many moves and holding alternative possibilities in mind as structures which the game may actually assume. In the consciousness of such a reader all eight of these questions and others, no doubt, must begin to take shape, along with emotional qualities which make answers to some seem more important than others—all in the few instants it takes him to read those first five words.

As the reading process continues, this reader's consciousness will be filing answers, dismissing apparent irrelevancies, framing new questions—developing a whole structure of intellectual and emotional expectations. Trying deliberately to make this process fully conscious—as it normally is not—we should be able to get some notion of how the opening of *The Unicorn* works on a responsive reader. After the first line the passage continues this way:

"Fifteen miles."
"Is there a bus?"
"There is not."
"Is there a taxi or car I can hire in the village?"
"There is not."
"Then how am I to get there?"
"You might hire a horse hereabouts," someone suggested after a silence.
"I can't ride a horse," she said in exasperation, "and in any case there's my luggage."

From this dialogue we begin inferentially to construct our notion of the situation and its future possibilities. We infer that the questioner is female, alone, in a strange place, come to stay for a while, probably arrived by train, certainly from a more urban place. She may have come to visit or to work. What she is doing in this obviously out-of-the-way place and why she is doing it become our larger tentative questions; exactly where is she going also insists on an answer; how she will get there remains a question but though immediate it does not seem vital, as we begin to assume she will somehow get there and our interest starts

to shift toward "there." In context the "it" of the first
sentence and the "there" of the seventh refer to something
that has been named earlier in the conversation. But since
we readers permanently lack that part of the conversation,
"it" and "there" are tantalizers that focus our inferential
activity toward a place already becoming mysterious for us.
The next paragraph gives further impetus to precisely this
phase of our ratiocination. In it we learn that the men who
have been replying to the questions, "while not exactly
hostile, entirely lacked the responsiveness of civilization.
They had looked at her a little strangely when she had told
them where she was going. Perhaps that was it." By this
point we have entered the consciousness of this female vis-
itor, we are sharing her perspective, and are especially
alerted by the ominous information in the last two sentences. There is something strange and forbidding about
the place where *we* (for now we are incorporated in *her*)
are going.

While all this local inferential activity is in progress, the
reader is also half-consciously commencing some vague blue-
prints for the entire structure. Even with no previous knowledge of Iris Murdoch, and with no clues from the jacket or
cover, the alert and experienced reader is given enough information in these opening lines so that his first, tentative
sketch should derive from his generic knowledge of sus-
pense-mystery fiction. Just as *The Lime Twig* makes use of
the conventions of hard-boiled American crime fiction, *The
Unicorn* uses the conventions of soft-boiled English mystery fiction. In both works the conventions provide a frame
of reference for the reader, helping him orient himself, but
they also provide material for ironic or parodic scrutiny by
the author, who manipulates the conventions with a cer-

tain amount of disdain. In *The Unicorn* Iris Murdoch shows her independence from the conventions of mystery fiction by gradually redirecting the alert reader from inferential activity on the level of who-dun-it and what'll-happen to a more abstract and philosophical level. She also toys with the conventions of comic pairing off of lovers and of tragic destruction of all the characters, and in doing so she transfers the reader's intellectual and emotional interest from the characters themselves to the ideas which have governed their actions. In *The Lime Twig* Hawkes proceeds differently, using his crime-story thread to string psychological rather than philosophical pearls, and letting his plot become clearer and more insistent as he goes along. Interestingly, both these works, in their titles, encourage ideation by naming objects which do not appear in the narratives. There is no lime twig in Hawkes's story and no unicorn in Iris Murdoch's. Both images offer us concepts that help to organize our perceptions into appropriate structures.

The process by which Iris Murdoch encourages us to shift our interest from the fictional to the ideational elements in her narrative is gradual. At certain points we are aware of a greater proportion of commentary to event, and I mean to single out some of these for special attention. But these points are merely climaxes in a structure of ideas which is just as narrative, just as dynamic, as the structure of pure event. For Iris Murdoch is teaching us how to read allegorically in *The Unicorn*, teasing us into this lost way of reading by almost imperceptibly moving from conventional mysteries of motivation and responsibility to the ideational mysteries of philosophy. She starts us building a "Gothic" structure of expectations and then, like a good guide, helps us to see that this fantastic edifice is not just another building with a pleasantly vertiginous view from the top, which gives us a delightful thrill. She allows us to discover that this work is "Gothic" like a cathedral in which every spire and every gargoyle is packed with meaningful allusions to an invisible world.

From "Gothic" action to "Gothic" allegory is the path we follow in this tale. To chart every step of the reader's imaginary journey, to watch in exquisite detail the visions and revisions through which his tentative plan for Strawberry Hill is revised to resemble Notre Dame—this might be worthwhile. It might also be tedious. And it would certainly require a book much longer than *The Unicorn* itself. Thus, in order to deal in some way with the relation between action and allegory in this work I must indulge in some short-cutting. So I ask my reader to assume the continuation of the inferential processes suggested by the foregoing consideration of the opening lines—through all thirty-five chapters of the book. The properly ratiocinative reader will emerge with a notion of the book's action something like the version I am about to reproduce. The following compact plot-summary should serve to symbolize the process of experiencing the story on the level of action; it should also help to provide that firm grip on the events of the plot which is indispensable for approaching the allegory; and it can function as a handy point of reference for the discussion of the story's meanings to come.

PART 1

Ch. 1. Marian Taylor, after an unhappy love affair, arrives at the remote village of Gaze to be a governess at Gaze Castle. She is met at the station by Gerald Scottow and young Jamesie Evercreech. On the ride to the Castle through desolate moors bordering a frightening coastline, she speculates on her exact duties and the positions of her two greeters. She sees the only other dwelling near Gaze Castle—Riders, home of the elderly scholar Max Lejour.

Ch. 2. Marian meets Violet Evercreech, Jamesie's sister, "practically his ma." She meets Denis Nolan, clerk at Gaze and keeper of the fishponds. Finally she meets the mistress of Gaze, Hannah Crean-Smith—an attractive, unkempt woman. Marian learns her "pupil" will not be a child but Hannah.

Ch. 3. Marian tries to swim in the cold sea but is afraid. On the shore she meets Alice Lejour, thirtyish daughter of Max, and learns that Alice's friend Effingham Cooper will be visiting Riders soon.

Ch. 4. Marian begins to teach Hannah French but puzzles over the feudal service Hannah receives from Denis and over Hannah's curiously convalescent and eccentric manner.

Ch. 5. Marian learns from Jamesie that Denis once worked at Riders but was chucked out because he "jumped" upon Alice. She also learns that Hannah's husband is alive, in New York, where he has been for seven years since he fell over a dreadful cliff near Gaze Castle.

Ch. 6. Marian senses and responds to Hannah's need for love.

Ch. 7. Marian meets Denis tending his fish. Denis tells her that seven years ago the brutal Peter Crean-Smith found Hannah in bed with young Philip (Pip) Lejour, and that shortly afterward he fell from the cliff in a struggle with Hannah. Since then Hannah has been a prisoner watched by Scottow and the Evercreeches. Marian sees herself as Gerald's adversary.

PART 2

Ch. 8. Effingham Cooper (who now divides with Marian the role of point-of-view character) comes to visit the Lejours. Max was his tutor at Oxford twenty years before. Alice has been in love with him for years, but he is a successful bureaucrat, with an accommodation with one of his female subordinates. Also, four years before on a visit to Max, he took refuge from a storm at Gaze, where he met Hannah and fell in love with her. His platonic adoration of Hannah has persisted.

Ch. 9. Effingham arrives at Riders where Pip, Alice, and Max are expecting something to happen because "It's seven years."

Ch. 10. Groups from Gaze and Riders meet while walking and hunting. Effingham meets Marian and agrees to help her learn Greek.

Ch. 11. Effingham pays a visit to Hannah, offers rescue, she declines.

Ch. 12. Effingham and Max talk about Hannah.

Ch. 13. Effingham learns from Pip that Gerald Scottow helped Pip and Hannah consummate their adulterous love seven years ago—and betrayed them to Peter.

Ch. 14. At a Greek lesson Marian tries unsuccessfully to persuade Effingham to rescue Hannah by abducting her.

PART 3

Ch. 15. Marian is asked by Violet Evercreech to "be kind" to Jamesie who "adores" her. Violet kisses Marian passionately. Marian thinks Jamesie might help rescue Hannah. In his room she finds pictures of Gerald unclothed and in "strange postures." Denis tells her Jamesie tried to rescue Hannah once and was caught by Gerald and whipped, afterwards becoming Gerald's "slave."

Ch. 16. At a musical evening Hannah bursts out weeping and Gerald agrees to help Marian rescue her.

Ch. 17. Marian and Effingham attempt the rescue by tricking Hannah into a car. As they near the gates a car driven by Alice drives them off the road. Then Gerald and Jamesie arrive.

Ch. 18. Gerald makes Marian promise not to try again, sealing the promise with a passionate kiss.

Ch. 19. Marian realizes she is now part of the family, the pattern. Alice reports Effingham has wandered into the bog.

PART 4

Ch. 20. Effingham has a metaphysical insight while close to death in the bog. Denis rescues him.

Ch. 21. Effingham rescued, dressed in Gerald's clothes, and fuddled by medicinal whisky tries to explain his insight to Hannah and the others. Gerald announces that Peter is returning to Gaze. Hannah pleads with Effingham to stay with her but Alice drags him away.

Ch. 22. Next evening Effingham returns to Gaze, to find Gerald carrying an apparently willing Hannah to his bedroom.

Ch. 23. The following morning Gerald announces that he is taking Hannah away. Alice reveals that long ago it was she who "sprang" upon Denis—not the reverse. Alice runs out.

Ch. 24. Effingham follows Alice, finds her in a weedy pool. They kiss.

PART 5

Ch. 25. Marian and Denis walk out to a salmon pool and make love.

Ch. 26. Effingham tells Marian he loves Alice. Word arrives that Peter is not coming after all.

Ch. 27. Hannah tells Marian that she (Hannah) has been playing God. Pip arrives at Gaze with a shotgun.

Ch. 28. Pip asks Hannah to come with him into the world. She refuses. He leaves. Gerald is master.

Ch. 29. Gerald, whom Denis says is becoming more like Peter, is killed by Hannah with a shotgun.

PART 6

Ch. 30. Violet and Jamesie take charge of Gaze, looking for Hannah's will and locking her in her room. Alice and Effingham decide to bring Max to Gaze for Peter's arrival.

Ch. 31. Hannah now wants to leave Gaze. Jamesie and Marian unlock her door and see her walk out.

Ch. 32. With rains continuing and flooding beginning Hannah's corpse is brought back to Gaze from "the rocks." Denis, who has gone to meet Peter, announces that Peter was drowned when the coast road flooded as they drove toward Gaze.

PART 7

Ch. 33. With the three bodies laid out in the drawing room, Max arrives and learns he is Hannah's heir.

Ch. 34. Marian and Denis part after he tells her that he caused Peter's death. He goes off through the bog to seek work at a "big house far beyond," taking his favorite fish with him. Alice sends his dog after him. Marian decides to return to the "real" world.

Ch. 35. Effingham parts from Alice and returns to the "real" world on the same train as Marian. Reading a paper he learns that Pip has "accidentally shot and killed himself while cleaning his gun." Effingham and Marian will talk the whole thing over.

From this level of event there are a number of paths leading to the ideational level of the narrative. The significance of the title cries out to be explored as it would not if the book had been called *The Mysterious Affair at Gaze*. Certain chapters in which there is little action indicated in the summary also seem to offer fertile areas for investigation: Chapter 12, for example. And even the simple plot-outline we are using here manages to suggest a significant difference between the worlds presented in the narrative. The world of Gaze and Riders is clearly differentiated from the "real" world outside. I mean to leave none of these avenues unexplored, but I want to begin with this notion of opposing worlds. If we can establish the general significance of these opposed worlds we should be able to proceed to further refinements of ideation.

This opposition, as I understand it, has much to do with our whole consideration of the uses of romance and fabulation; for Marian and Effingham come from the "real" world into Gaze just as we readers come into a work of fiction. Just as we do, they make ethical choices and participate in events which leave them unscathed, though the fictional world is strewn with corpses as the curtain is drawn upon it. But they are not entirely unchanged though they have escaped. Marian, now, will "dance at Geoffrey's wedding." The sorrow and heaviness which drove her into the world of fabulation have been removed by her vicarious existence at Gaze, and she can return rejoiced and refreshed to the confusion and ordinariness in which real people are obliged to exist. All this seems far from accidental. *The Unicorn* is, on its esthetic level, a fabulator's manifesto, in which the book itself is seen as fulfilling the purifying function of the traditional scapegoat, by providing a ritual purgation for those initiated into its mysteries.

Marian and Effingham, then, through whose eyes we view the events at Gaze, are representatives of our point of view. They come from the world of realism into a world of romance. They are, like Lockwood in *Wuthering Heights*, necessary intermediaries between these two worlds. (And, like Lockwood, they are both getting away from unsatisfactory erotic relationships in the world they have left.) But in this narrative they also embody certain "modern" ideas and attitudes which collide, in the course of events, with the values prevailing in the world of Gaze and Riders. Marian and Effingham believe in a set of liberal, enlightened virtues: freedom, individual responsibility, personal choice. Like most of us, they have derived their values from a mixture of neo-Freudian hedonism and easygoing utilitarianism. They are for Life and against Death, and they view life as mainly a matter of the senses. These

values, to which most enlightened modern citizens sub-
scribe, are met and tested in the story by the events at
Gaze. In this castle a more medieval and feudal set of values prevails. Furthermore, a chain of events is in progress
—variously referred to by Marian as a "story" or a "pattern" which seems like something out of a medieval romance. A *princesse lointaine* (as Effingham's devoted
friend in the "real" world calls Hannah) is actually being
held prisoner as if under a spell maintained by a distant
magician. And all these doings are watched from Riders
where a philosopher (Max), a poet (Pip), and a gardener
(Alice) live an apparently simple, classical life. Riders,
dominated by Max's Platonic or Socratic vision, seems actually to represent a third perspective in the narrative: that
of ancient wisdom. Thus we have something like these
three basic matrices:

Marian and Effingham = modern "self-development"
The Gaze household = feudal Christianity
The Riders household = classical Platonism.

Deriving from these primary allegorical elements are various individual refinements manifested in the characters,
and these refinements of ideation are complicated and
qualified by the collisions and couplings of characters as
the action proceeds.

At the center of the story is Hannah. The allegory
turns mainly on the meaning of her life—the events in it
and her reactions to them. Because she is at the center, she
is the most remote from us. We see her mainly from the
points of view of Marian and Effingham, the outsiders who
enter the charmed circle of her love. Marian's perspective
on Hannah is widened by Denis, with whom she discusses
Hannah's situation. Denis, who serves Hannah with un-

questioning feudal devotion is a religious man, a believer. Our first extended insight into the allegorical implications of the story comes in Chapters 6 and 7, during Marian's talks with Hannah and Denis. Marian is firmly committed to *this* world. In Chapter 6 she and Hannah discuss religion. Marian "never went to church." She is surprised to find Hannah religious. They discuss love, Hannah begging Marian's pardon "for so shamelessly crying out for love." Hannah moves easily from love to religion: "Yet we all need love. Even God needs love. I suppose that's why He created us." Marian's dry comment is, "He made a bad arrangement." Later she questions Hannah's love of God: "But suppose you're loving—something that isn't there?" Hannah's reply leads toward mystical Platonism: "In a way you can't love something that isn't there. I think if you really love, then something *is* there. But I don't understand these things." If Marian is a modern "realist," Hannah is a medieval one. Hannah accepts the reality of universals, the priority of mind over matter.

In Chapter 7, Marian and Denis talk about Hannah. Denis tells Marian that the local people believe Hannah to be under a curse: "They believe that if she comes out of the garden she will die." Moreover, Denis adds, "They think that at the end of seven years something will happen to her." The conversation continues this way:

"Why seven years? Just because that's the time things go on for in fairy tales? But it is the end of seven years now!"
"Yes. But nothing is going to happen."
"Something has happened. I have come."
He was silent, as if shrugging his shoulders.
"Why have I come?" said Marian. Her own place in the story occurred to her for the first time. The ghastly tale had become a

reality all about her, it was still going on. And it was a tale in which nothing happened at random.

Several aspects of this passage require attention. The last paragraph presents Marian seeing herself as entering a "tale" which has materialized around her: a tale in which nothing happens at random. This is, of course, strictly true in an ironic way. Marian is a character in a tale by Iris Murdoch, who is certainly the God of this little fictional universe—a very careful God, who will let nothing happen at random. But the passage raises the further question of Marian's role in this tale she has entered. The tale of Hannah is believed to be reaching a crucial stage. And Marian's arrival, her entering the tale at this point, must be significant: "Something has happened. I have come." A few paragraphs later she decides to accept her role in the story. She and Denis have tried unsuccessfully to guess who arranged for Gerald Scottow to hire her in the first place. They do not reach a conclusion about this, but Marian decides to give a meaning of her own to her presence at Gaze:

> A prophetic flash of understanding burned her with terrible warmth. That was what she was for; she was for Gerald Scottow: his adversary, his opposite angel. By wrestling with Scottow she would make her way into the story. It was scarcely a coherent thought and it was gone in a moment.

Some of the irony involved in this resolution of Marian's should be apparent from the plot-summary. The rest, I shall return to later on. Her conversation with Denis continues, however, and we hear her sounding the typical notes of her modern, enlightened view of things. She can domesticate this mystery by reducing it to psychological terms:

"It sounds to me as if she were really under a spell, I mean a psychological spell, half believing by now that she's somehow *got* to stay here. Oughtn't she to be wakened up? I mean it's all so unhealthy, so unnatural."

"What is spiritual is unnatural. The soul under the burden of sin cannot flee. What is enacted here with her is enacted with all of us in one way or another. You cannot come between her and her suffering, it is too complicated, too precious. We must play her game, whatever it is, and believe her beliefs. That is all we can do for her."

"Well, it's not what I'm going to do," said Marian. "I'm going to talk to her about freedom."

Denis urges Marian not to trouble Hannah with freedom since she seems to have "made her peace with God" and accepted her punishment.

The other direct perspective we have on Hannah is Effingham's. Like Marian, he tries to take a modern and enlightened view of things. He, too, is in love with Hannah. And just as Denis qualifies Marian's perspective with his feudal and religious view of Hannah, Max Lejour qualifies Effingham's perspective with his Platonic view. Chapters 11 and 12 parallel 6 and 7 in the structure of the book. In Chapter 11 Effingham has *his* serious interview with Hannah. In Chapter 12 he discusses her with Max. When he sees her she seems "lovelier than ever," but "no younger." He observes that "something was written on that brow, something about suffering: only he could not read the characters." Like Marian, he wants to "break this spell." Hannah responds to his offer of rescue (he would restore her to "ordinary life") by regretting that she has let him into her extraordinary existence: "If it were *now* I think I would send you away, I would not let such a story begin at all." Effingham parts from her, after gazing into "her big golden eyes. She was marvelously strange to him, a fey, almost demonic creature sometimes."

Effingham returns to Riders (Chapter 12) dreading Max's Socratic interrogation. But we, the readers, look forward to it. The mysteriousness of things has been getting intolerable, and we are anxious for more light. Max seems obviously designed to help us, for unlike Denis, he is not involved in these events. And if we distrust the simple theology of Denis, we hope for more from the philosophy of Max. From a philosopher named Lejour, surely, we are entitled to expect light. And Max provides some: the best and clearest we get in working our way through this dark conceit. But Effingham is a man of intelligence too, and his perceptions undercut some of Max's. Moreover, Max himself declares, "I wish I understood more." Final answers are not going to be provided for us in this book. It is a *modern* allegory.

Max and Effingham first clash over Effingham's attempt to draw a political allegory from his visit to Gaze: the police state of Gaze *vs.* the free society of Riders. Max replies:

"The free society? That rag freedom! Freedom may be a value in politics but it's not a value in morals. Truth, yes. But not freedom. That's a flimsy idea, like happiness. In morals we are all prisoners, but the name of our cure is not freedom."

All prisoners, thought Effingham. Speak for yourself, old man. You are a prisoner of books, age, and ill health. It then occurred to him that in some curious way Max might derive consolation from the spectacle, over there in the other house, of another captivity, a distorted mirror image of his own.

It is possible to gloss this passage with the observation that neither Gaze nor Riders is free because they are both devoted to an ideal world: Gaze to a medieval mystery of suffering and obedience; Riders to the Socratic abstractions Goodness, Truth, and Beauty. For the reader, the values of Gaze, Riders, and the "real" world become clearer and clearer as he goes along. But the question of which set is "right" seems to become more and more elusive. Hannah seems to mean something different to everybody, and the reader who carries his mystery-story set of expectations over into the ideational complexities of *The Unicorn* longs for the dénouement. Gradually, one realizes that this is just what Iris Murdoch is not going to provide. The relativity of significance emanating from Hannah's suffering is in itself a major dimension of the book's meaning. This book is partly about the difficulty of settling on The Truth in the twentieth century. But if a Truth and a Meaning are elusive, meanings are not. In this discussion between Max and Effingham, Iris Murdoch allows Max to make a number of choral statements which refine our understanding of the meanings attached to Hannah and her suffering. Max says,

"In a way we can't help using her as a scapegoat. In a way that's what she's for, and to recognize it is to do her honour. She is our image of the significance of suffering. But we must also see her as real. And that will make us suffer too."

"I'm not sure that I understand," said Effingham. "I know one mustn't think of her as a legendary creature, a beautiful unicorn—"

"The unicorn is also the image of Christ. But we have to do with an ordinary guilty person."

The book's title makes this passage important. And the passage emphasizes the medieval and allegorical quality of the whole work. Max's statement that the "unicorn is also the image of Christ" is a bit of medieval typology. The medieval bestiaries tell us that "Our Lord Jesus Christ is also a Unicorn spiritually." Specifically, the unicorn's small stature (as the bestiaries describe him) is associated with the humility of the Lord in assuming flesh. The unicorn's curious affinity for maidens (hunters cannot catch one except by leading a virgin girl to where the beast lurks, whereupon it leaps into the girl's lap and embraces her) is associated with the virgin birth of Christ. And finally (in the words of a twelfth-century bestiary translated by T. H. White) "It is like a kid or scapegoat because the Saviour himself was made in the likeness of sinful flesh, and from sin he condemned sin." That Hannah, as the unicorn of the title, is some sort of Christ figure, seems born out in her name, Crean-Smith, which is an anagram for Christ-name or Christ-mean. But her first name, which reads the same backwards as forwards, suggests a duplicity or ambiguity in the significance of her life which the connection with Christ does not resolve for modern audiences. This is precisely the point at which the modern allegory is to be distinguished from the medieval. The Hannah = Christ equation in a medieval work would function mainly in one direction, with the character Hannah acquiring an unearthly dignity by means of the allegory. But in this modern work that process, though it operates, is counterbalanced by a flow of ideation in the opposite direction. The ambiguity of Hannah's position works to undercut and make relative the Christian view of the cosmos. The equation of the modern allegory does not say that Hannah's suffering is significant because it is a type of Christ's. It says that Hannah's suffering and Christ's are equally significant, and the significance depends on what we believe about it.

Max, in fact, offers Effingham an interpretation of Hannah's situation which is a pagan parallel to the Christian view. He sees the Greek concept of Até as relevant to Hannah: "the almost automatic transfer of suffering from one being to another" which "is finally quenched when it encounters a pure being who only suffers and does not attempt to pass the suffering on." But when Effingham asks whether Max really considers Hannah such a being, Max can only reply that she may be, or she may be quite the opposite—a "sort of enchantress, a Circe, a spiritual Penelope keeping her suitors spellbound and enslaved." Then the discussion ranges over Max's own ethics, including his criticism of relativistic "existentialists and linguistic philosophers" who vulgarize the unimaginable nature of the Good by making it "into a mere matter of personal choice." At one point, he comes very close to the view of the absolute expressed by Hannah in Chapter 6, only where she made her formulation in religious terms (God exists if you believe in him) he makes his in ethical, quoting " 'Desire and possession of the Good are one.' " Finally, however, Max admits the subjective limitations of his own view of the situation:

"Perhaps Hannah is my experiment! I've always had a great theoretical knowledge of morals, but practically speaking I've never done a hand's turn. . . . I don't know the truth either. I just know about it."

Thus we are given quantities of food for ratiocination in Chapter 12, but no single, clearly acceptable interpretation of events. We are left, with a handful of clues, to continue developing a tentative structure of meanings for ourselves.

Effingham is as reluctant to accept Max's view of the possible significance of passive suffering, just as Marian was reluctant to accept Denis's Christian formulation of the same position. Both Max and Denis seem to accept the traditional view that though the individual has not made the world and has little control over its operation, he is nevertheless responsible for what goes on within his reach. Marian and Effingham, on the other hand, speak for those modern moralists who see the individual as hardly responsible for anything but blessed with all sorts of freedom. Consider the confusions and cross-purposes implicit in these thoughts of Marian's in Chapter 15:

She felt above all, as a sort of *categorical imperative*, the desire to set Hannah free, to smash up all her eerie magical surroundings, *to let the fresh air in at last:* even if the result should be some dreadful suffering.

I have italicized that Kant phrase of modern morality, the *categorical imperative*, to point up its presence in Marian's thought. The categorical imperative is, as has been observed, an attempt to generate an absolute and systematic morality without justification from the invisible world: "old Kant's Tartuffery" Nietzsche called it. The other phrase I have italicized harks back to Ibsenism, echoing Lona's ringing curtain speech in Act I of *The Pillars of Society*. It reminds us that Marian *is* a kind of Ibsenite "new woman," independent, aggressive, free. But she has wandered into a morality play in which freedom and pleasure contend with such antagonistic virtues as submission and endurance. The categorical command to be free is itself a paradoxical imperative, because freedom means absence of command; it cannot be imposed. Marian's actions in this morality play take on allegorical significance, then, as an exploration of the limitations of this existential paradox. She enlists Effingham and tries to abduct Hannah. She will end Hannah's expiatory suffering by forcing freedom upon her, "even if the result should be some dreadful suffering."

Marian herself, of course, is far from free. Not only is she the servant of her absolute faith in freedom; she is also the instrument of other powers. She sees herself as Gerald Scottow's adversary. But after the escape has failed Gerald rewards her with a lecture, a kiss, and the nickname of "Maid Marian." In the kiss, she realizes, she has submitted: "Gerald could have had anything he wanted in that dark bedroom." In the lecture he offers a stoical and deterministic view of the world:

"There are things which are appalling to young people because young people think life should be happy and free. But life is never really happy and free in any beautiful sense. Happiness is a weak and paltry thing, and perhaps 'freedom' has no meaning. There are great patterns in which we are all involved, and destinies which belong to us and which we love even in the moment when they destroy us."

He adds that "the pattern" is what has "absolute authority" in the world of Gaze—"here." In the pattern, she and Gerald are not so much adversaries as accomplices. Their opposition is necessary for the ends of the pattern to be accomplished.

Marian's new title, *Maid Marian*, is even more interesting. The bestiaries tell us that the Unicorn can be trapped only by a virgin girl used as a lure. And they liken Mary, mother of Jesus, to this virgin because she is the medium through which perfect divinity enters the sinful world of flesh. Our Maid Marian is the virgin lure. Through her intercession Hannah has been entangled in a new web of circumstance which will result in her undertaking a renewed burden of sin and guilt. Maid Marian herself is

destined to stain her immaculate innocence in the pattern
of events she has entered. When she boldly tells Denis,
"Something has happened. I have come," the major irony
of her words lies in her ignorance of the role she has been
cast for in this mystery play. In Chapter 15, when Denis
tells her, "Everyone here is involved in guilt," the reply
she murmurs half to herself is, "Except me. Except me.
Except me." But by Chapter 19 she is beginning to learn
her part: "I have become a part of the pattern," she thinks,
later adding that she is "involved now." Finally, when she
helps to set Hannah free to die in Chapter 31, she is no
longer an innocent maid involved without knowing it in a
plot to catch a unicorn. She sees this act as one of "blood
guilt which would make its own reckoning." And she has
doubts about the rightness of her act. No more easy categorical imperatives absolve her from the difficulties of personal decision:

Had she done right to give Hannah this last thing, the freedom to
make her life over in her own way into her own property? When at
last Hannah had wanted to break the mirror, to go out through
the gate, ought she *then* to have been her jailer? It was not any
more the old images of freedom which could move her now. It was
Hannah's authority which had moved her, her sense, in the pathetic
scene of her final imprisonment, of Hannah's sovereignty, of her
royal right to dispose of herself as she would.

Instead of imposing "freedom" Marian is now admitting
the divine right of other people to make their own choices.
And she is willing to accept the responsibility for allowing
Hannah this choice. Recognizing her guilt, she expects her
punishment to follow: "And now she stood, as it were, in
Hannah's place, and it was perhaps on her that the axe
would fall." But in Chapter 34 Marian finds that she will

not, after all, be "in Hannah's place." That painful crux is reserved for Denis, whose action in being unfaithful to Hannah (both by making love to Marian and by losing faith in the significance of Hannah's suffering) and in deliberately killing Peter (another breach of faith) has made him the "most guilty." Denis tells Marian that in his guilt lies her "cure."

"I should have loved only and not hated at all. I should have stayed by her and suffered all with her, beside her, becoming her. There was really no other way and I knew that before. But I let myself be driven mad by jealousy, and by her actions, and I was faithless to her and so became mad. I am the most guilty. The guilt passes to me. That is why I must go away by myself."

"But does that leave me—free?"

Denis does not answer Marian's question, but she finally understands that his acceptance of guilt does leave her free. "Yes," she says to him, "you are becoming Hannah now." Denis is the new unicorn, the new scapegoat, the new saviour who takes upon himself the sins of others to atone for them. With the departure of Denis, Marian has a "sense of it all beginning again, the whole tangled business: the violence, the prison house, the guilt. It all still existed. Yet Denis was taking it away with him." Finally, however, she is not sure of the meaning of her experience in this "other world" which she has visited:

. . . she did not know whether the world in which she had been living was a world of good or of evil, a world of significant suffering or a devil's shadow-play, a mere nightmare of violence.

And neither do we.

Like Denis and Marian, Max and Effingham have their final views of the matter. And we have our final views of them. Unlike Denis and Marian, Max and Effingham have kept clear of the final action. Effingham has had his metaphysical vision while sinking into the bog—surely an allegory of the absurdity of thought divorced from action. And Max has watched and thought. These two have not become involved in guilt. But they are responsible for their inactions. Max is Hannah's heir, as philosophy is the heir of theology: "Max will speak her funeral speech, Max will tell the world what she was," thinks Effingham jealously. And Max interprets this gesture of Hannah's as a "romantic decision—if you like, a symbolic decision." He insists that Hannah, "like the rest of us" loved "what wasn't there." And he adds that she "could not really love the people she saw." Here Alice interrupts to tell her father that *he* was the one person she could have loved in presence. To this Max has no response but a shake of the head. But Effingham insists that Max is "her death, and she loved you." Interpretations begin piling up. Max turns Hannah into a symbol, an idea. Earlier Effingham had turned her into a Freudian notion (Chapter 30)—the chaste mother figure desired by the jealous child. Seen this way, Hannah's acceptance of Gerald Scottow as a lover broke the spell of Effingham's "courtly love" for her and freed him to make love to Alice; just as it freed Denis and Marian to perform the act of love. Hannah's "faithlessness" was mirrored by that of those who loved her.

Hannah herself presents an interpretation of her life before its catastrophe. In Chapter 27 she says that she has been playing the part of God but she is really "nothing, a legend." And she adds that

"It was your belief in the significance of my suffering that kept me going. Ah, how much I needed you all! I have battened upon

you like a secret vampire. I have even battened on Max Lejour."
She sighed. "I needed my audience, I lived in your gaze like a false
God. But it is the punishment of a false God to become unreal. I
have become unreal. You have made me unreal by thinking about
me so much. You made me an object of contemplation. Just like
this landscape. I have made it unreal by endlessly looking at it."

This passage must certainly qualify some of the other views
presented. It comes, so to speak, from the unicorn's mouth.
In particular, the orthodox Christian view of Hannah's
death adopted by Denis and Marian, though it follows this
speech and Hannah's death, cannot be seen as the last
word, the one true interpretation of the events at Gaze. "I
lived in your gaze"—says Hannah. The world of Gaze is a
place where order, system, and meaning all exist because
they are imposed from without. They are in the eyes of the
beholders.

   In this book, then, we are not entitled to make any final
choice among the various metaphysical possibilities of-
fered us. But the book is far from meaningless. There is a
meaning in its lesson in relativity. And there is a further
meaning, I believe, in our final views of Marian and Effingham. Hannah's view of herself is echoed by Effingham's
last thoughts of her as he heads back toward "reality" in
the train. He thinks of her as a "strange nun" and agrees
that Max was right in saying that they had all

turned towards her to discover a significance in their own sufferings,
to load their own evil into her to be burned up. It had been a
fantasy of the spiritual life, a story, a tragedy. Only the spiritual
life has no story and is not tragic. Hannah had been for them an
image of God; and if she was a false God they had certainly
worked hard to make her so. He thought of her now as a doomed
figure, a Lilith, a pale death-dealing enchantress: anything but a
human being.

Finally, he decides that "if what was over had indeed been a fantasy of the spiritual life, it was its fantastic and not its spiritual quality which had touched him." Effingham and Marian, as they leave the world of spiritual fantasy and head toward the "familiar ordinary world" suggest two kinds of readers and two ways of encountering a book like *The Unicorn*, which is itself a "fantasy of the spiritual life": the reader who, like Marian, becomes engaged in the events and touches good and evil through imaginative experience; and the reader who, like Effingham, remains aloof "through egoism, through being in some sense too small." The Effinghamish reader will find only a fantasy in *The Unicorn*. The Marianite will be touched and moved spiritually. The Effinghamish critic, in particular, will discourse glibly about such a book. He will be detached, amusing, skeptical. He will be more judicious than the Marianite, perhaps. But he will lack one thing: that experience of the story which can come only to the reader who commits himself to it imaginatively. Which is the right way? As in larger issues, Iris Murdoch leaves us to choose. But I think I know which choice she feels we should make.

CHAPTER **6** FABULATION AND EPIC VISION

I A SACRED BOOK

Is it true that our air is disturbed, as Mallarmé said, by "the trembling of the veil of the temple" or "that our whole age is seeking to bring forth a sacred book?" Some of us thought that book near toward the end of the last century, but the tide sank.

(W. B. Yeats in *The Trembling of the Veil*)

The *fin de siècle* was pleasantly titillated by intimations of Apocalypse. But in our time the holocaust is too real a possibility to be considered with a *symboliste frisson*. The veil of the temple has blown away entirely, and we can hear something ticking in there. The fragmentation Yeats perceived as the curse of modern civilization has continued; the center holds together even less than it did. But we have got our sacred book now. In the midst of our tribulations *Giles Goat-Boy* has slouched toward Buffalo to be born. Hallelujah!

John Barth's fourth work of fiction is a tract for our

135

times, an epic to end all epics, and a sacred book to end all sacred books. It is not, I hasten to say, a merely blasphemous work of empty nihilism, though some reviewers have reacted as if it were. It is a work of genuine epic vision, a fantastic mosaic constructed from the fragments of our life and traditions, calculated to startle us into new perceptions of the epic hero and saviour. It is epic in its scope: in its combination of myth and history, of the ideal and the actual. And it is a sacred book because it is concerned with the life of a religious hero and with the way to salvation. True, it treats these matters comically, even farcically at times; and it is militantly fabulative, insisting on its fabulous dimension, its unreality. But this insistence is part of the book's point: In our time any sacred book must be a work of fiction.

Barth's choice of comic allegory as the method of his fiction should come as no surprise to anyone who has read *The Fabulators* from the beginning. The vision of fabulation is essentially comic because it is an instrument of reason; and it is frankly allegorical because it has not the naïve faith in the possibility of capturing the actual world on the printed page which realism requires of its practitioners. Barth has observed that

If you are a novelist of a certain type of temperament, then what you really want to do is reinvent the world. God wasn't too bad a novelist, except he was a Realist.

Realism, in this view, is a game that only God can play. Man is not in a position to recreate God's world on paper. The old realistic novel has always assumed that a readily ascertainable thing called reality exists, and that we all live in it; therefore, it is the only thing to write about. But

Barth says that he doesn't "know much about Reality." He declines the realistic gambit, refuses to accept the notion that the truth can be captured just by reporting the way things are. Barth insists on an inevitable "discrepancy between art and the Real Thing." His comment on the French *nouveau roman* is enlightening:

From what I know of Robbe-Grillet and his pals, their aesthetic is finally a more up-to-date kind of psychological realism: a higher fi to human consciousness and unconsciousness. Well, that's nice. A different way to come to terms with the discrepancy between art and the Real Thing is to *affirm* the artificial element in art (you can't get rid of it anyhow), and make the artifice part of your point instead of working for higher and higher fi with a lot of literary woofers and tweeters. That would be my way. Scheherazade's my *avant-gardiste*.

The Real Thing, then, is God's world. The world of the fabulator is different. And the difference, the artifice, is "part of your point." The fabulator's attitude toward life is elliptical. By presenting something that is like life but markedly different from it, he helps us to define life by indirection. Fabulation is a tricky business for both reader and writer—a matter of delicate control on the one hand and intelligent inference on the other. Any reader of *Giles Goat-Boy*, then, will be put on his mettle. The demands on his learning and ingenuity will be strenuous.

II "GILES GOAT-BOY": SCOPES AND VISION

In *Giles Goat-Boy*, John Barth has forged an allegorical instrument that enables him to piece together our fragmented world and explore the possible ways of living in it. To understand the vision of this book the reader must come

to terms with its allegory. He must learn its workings—
its facets and their relations; in fact he must discover how
to play his part in the interpretation of the events of the
story. Thus, for the bulk of this chapter I shall be concerned with mastery of the allegorical dimensions of the
story. But before trying to thread the entire labyrinth of
the allegory, I think it advisable to make a sort of preliminary sortie to determine whether the game is worth
the candle. We can begin to assess the value of a literary
work by considering closely some representative passages.
This is a dangerous business, and can be grossly unfair,
especially in dealing with a work like this one, which is
highly structured and depends for its cumulative effect
upon the careful dovetailing of many thematic and narrative elements. But Barth is asking a good deal of his
readers in the way of a commitment of time and energy, so
he must be ready to let us do a bit of preliminary examining before making the big plunge.

The passages I have selected for investigation should
provide some sense of the texture of Barth's prose, and
the way his vision is related to his use of language. Moreover, since they are thematically related, they should reveal
something of the book's structure as well. Each passage is
concerned directly with vision, and with the use of scopes
or lenses as visual aids. Just as the ubiquitous mirrors of the
Alexandria Quartet emphasized that work's cubist per-
spectivism, so does a bizarre collection of scopes and lenses
underscore the motifs of quest and perception in *Giles
Goat-Boy*. The first passage is a description of a tender
moment. After many trials and tribulations, the hero holds
the heroine in his arms:

"Anastasia . . ." The name seemed strange to me now, and her hair's rich smell. What was it I held called *Anastasia?* A slender bagful of meaty pipes and pouches, grown upon with hairs, soaked through with juices, strung up on jointed sticks, the whole thing pulsing, squirting, bubbling, flexing, combusting, and respiring in my arms; doomed soon enough to decompose into its elements, yet afflicted in the brief meanwhile with mad imaginings, so that, not content to jelly through the night and meld, ingest, divide, it troubled its sleep with dreams of passèdness, of *love*. . . .

Obviously, this is no ordinary love scene. The hero has some excuse for his anatomical ruminations, however, since he has just finished gazing at the lady's innards through a fluoroscope. The scene continues:

She squeezed more tightly; I felt the blood-muscle pumping behind her teat, through no governance of *Anastasia.* My penis rose unbid by *George;* was it a George of its own? A quarter-billion beasties were set to swarm therefrom and thrash like salmon up the mucous of her womb; were they little Georges all?
I groaned: "I don't understand anything!" (p. 616)

We might call the vision here fluoroscopic. It penetrates the skin to the meaty pipes and pouches within. But it also looks at the outsides of the human anatomy. And it listens as well, even noting chemical processes such as the combustion which turns fodder into energy, warming the human frame. This embrace in a doctor's office is presented in appropriately clinical terminology, but the language is not merely clinical. In particular the verbal drive of the passage is remarkable. Consider these verbal forms from a single sentence: "grown upon . . . soaked through . . . strung up . . . pulsing, squirting, bubbling, flexing, combusting, and respiring . . . doomed . . . to decompose . . . afflicted . . . to jelly . . . meld . . . ingest . . . di-

vide . . . troubled." These verb forms alone, excerpted
from the sentence in which they function, illustrate the
range and precision of Barth's vocabulary. Together they
emphasize the complexity of mere organic existence, the
multifariousness of the life process. And all the participles
and infinitives which describe this complexity weigh against
the main verb of the sentence, which comes at the end—
"troubled." Despite its ineluctably physical mechanisms,
described so richly and fully, this organism, this human
body, this Anastasia *troubles* its mere mechanical existence
with ideals—notions that no fluoroscope or microscope can
locate or justify, dreams of blessedness and love. Moreover,
in addition to these ideals, which trouble the organism and
keep it from merely jellying along like an amoeba, the body
is swayed and governed by all sorts of corporeal activity beyond its control and beyond that necessary for its untrou-
bled existence—the heart pounding, where it need only
beat; the penis rising, yearning toward another. Where in
all this mixture of activity and purpose does the identity of
Anastasia or of George begin and end, the passage asks.
And the quarter-billion spermatozoa ready to thrash salm-
on-like about their master's business—who are they? And
who is their master?

One of George's mysterious tasks, which he must achieve
in order to complete his heroic quest, is to "see through
your ladyship." The fluoroscopic method reveals some
things, but it provides no final illumination, only riddles
—especially riddles of the sphincter. This passage must
be contrasted with the act of love later performed by
George and Anastasia in the belly of the great computer,
which is the true fulfillment of the task. (And this act
itself must be contrasted with George's first non-human

"servicing" of Anastasia—the televised Sunrise Service performed in Stoker's Living Room as the climax to his great vernal orgy.) The act of love is the necessary act of vision for George, because when we simply look, no matter how fine our scope, we merely (like Max Lejour in *The Unicorn*) "know about" the things we gaze at. When we act, and engage ourselves with things, we come to know them. In WESCAC's belly George knows Anastasia as Adam knew Eve. And she conceives. In a way Barth is exploring the truth in the linguistic riddles posed by words like "know" and "conceive." And he is using the action of his fiction to expound a philosophy of action which cannot properly be presented discursively. Any commentary on this fictional action—such as mine, here—amounts to reducing "knowing" to "knowing about." All interpretive criticism amounts to this. That is the limitation of such criticism. And one of its virtues—clarification—is a function of this limitation. It clarifies, at the expense of reducing the experience of fiction, through which we "know" a work, to a discussion through which we "know about" it. Thus its only use is to prepare us to encounter or re-encounter the primary material, the work itself.

Having looked at a passage of fluoroscopic vision, and considered briefly its place in the whole scheme, we may now turn to a passage which connects the limited sphere of proctoscopy to a more cosmic view of things. This passage, from early in the book, presents the achievement of George's tutor, Max Spielman. In it we can find the same disposition in Barth to explore the riddle of language, to shake the hidden meanings out of metaphors, and to use puns and other devices of language as ways to generate new meanings:

In three words Max Spielman synthesized all the fields which thitherto he'd browsed in brilliantly one by one—showed the "sphincter's riddle" and the mystery of the University to be the same. *Ontogeny recapitulates cosmogeny*—what is it but to say that proctoscopy repeats hagiography? That our Founder on Founder's Hill and the rawest freshman on his first *mons veneris* are father and son? That my day, my year, my life, and the history of West Campus are wheels within wheels? (p. 7)

Like Joyce in *Finnegans Wake*, Barth is playing with archetypes here, and playing with words. It was Oedipus who solved the sphinx's riddle and became the saviour of his city. And it was Oedipus who killed his father, married his mother, and finally saved his city once again by becoming a scapegoat, suffering expulsion and blindness to atone for his lack of vision. By the punning alteration of *sphinx's* to *sphincter's*, Barth unites these two actions more firmly than Freud himself, and in doing so he brings whole mansions of philosophy into the place of excrement. The sphincter's riddle involves the mysteries of creation and of love. That portion of feminine anatomy so beautifully named the mount of Venus provides both linguistic and archetypal connections to those mountains of mythology where the high god performs his creative act, making a cosmos out of chaos. Barth has taken the Darwinian "ontogeny recapitulates philogeny"—the life of the individual organism in its growth stages repeats the evolutionary cycle of its species—he has taken this and substituted "cosmogeny" for "philogeny," turning biology into archetypology. The mystery of the universe and the sphincter's riddle are the same because the genesis of the individual and the genesis of the cosmos are aspects of the same process. The proctoscope examining fundamental human anatomy will tell us the same thing as the lives of the saints: because saints, too, have fundaments, and because—though the place *is* the place of excrement—the mansions of love and creative power are indubitably there. The greatness of Max Spielman is in seeing the connection. That is epic vision.

The fluoroscope of Dr. Sear, the proctoscope of Max Spielman—these fallible gadgets are closer to seeing into the mystery of the universe than the telescopes and other lenses of Eblis Eierkopf. According to Eierkopf, Spielman "thinks with his ventricles." And Sear's main locus of thought seems even lower in the human anatomy than the heart. But Eierkopf, as his name suggests, is all eye and head. He is so much the man of "reason," in fact, that he cannot perform the simplest bodily functions without aid from the nearly brainless but superbly physical Croaker. When Eierkopf is mounted on Croaker's shoulders, together they make something like a whole man. But Eierkopf by himself represents a purely scientific and positivistic approach to the mystery of the universe. All his lenses —from his great telescope down to his eyeglasses—are designed by Barth to expose the limits of this kind of vision. He watches coeds undress with an infra-red telescope in his frivolous moments, but this is not so much wicked as it is revealing: revealing of Eierkopf, that is, for he watches nature in the same way: "*I try to take nature by surprise.*" And what he is looking for is a miracle. He denies the world of spirit in this way:

". . . You want spooks and spirits? Bah, George Goat-Boy! We look with our microscopes and our telescopes, and what do we see? Order! Number! Energies and Elements! Where's any Founder or Grand Tutor?" He tapped his gleaming skull. "In here, no place else. . . ."

But in his weaker moments he hopes with his gazing and peering to find something else:

". . . *I try to take nature by surprise!* I try to catch her napping once!" He laughed at his own folly, which it nevertheless plainly excited him to confess. He would sometimes stare at the furniture of his observatory for hours on end, he declared, at the familiar books and instruments in their accustomed places, and contemplate the inexorable laws of nature that held them fast, determined their appearance and relations, and governed his perception of them. And he would find himself first fretting that the brown pencil-jar on his desk, for example, could not suddenly turn green, or stir of its own volition; from a fret that such wonders could not be, he would come to a wish that just once they might, thence to a vain and gruntsome willing that they be—as if by concentration he could bring a miracle to pass. (pp. 335–6)

In the final dramatic scene at Max's shafting, Eierkopf becomes a believer in the matter of Grand Tutoriality:

"I'm *Übertrittig*, Goat-Boy!" he cried, "My eyes have been opened!" . . . For he had seen with his own two eyes (abetted, to be sure, by corrective lenses) wonders unexplainable by natural law and student reason.

The wonders he has seen, however, have been performed by George's devilish adversary, Harold Bray. Eierkopf's positivistic science has led him to embrace evil as the supreme good. The devil cannot only quote scripture if he needs to. He can also appear to defy natural law in such a way as to make those who demand only ocular evidence of divinity take him for a god. Which is just what Eblis Eierkopf does. The eye-ball, too, is a lens, and vision is not just a matter of eye-balls. That is one of the lessons of the Oedipus myth. Oedipus sees truly only after he is blind. This myth, and Dante's mythic trip through Hell and Purgatory to Paradise, have contributed heavily to Barth's vision in *Giles Goat-Boy*. Just as Dante must learn to abandon reason for revelation when reason has taken him as far as it can, leaving his old guide, Vergil, for his new one, Beatrice; so George, separated from his mentor, Max, gains his greatest insight when he sees through his lady-ship: in the dark of WESCAC's belly, his head covered by his mother's purse and his body united with Anastasia's in conjugal embrace, he sees: "In the darkness, blinding light! The end of the University! Commencement Day!"

III   THE ALLEGORICAL VISION OF "GILES GOAT-BOY"

A. *Basic Metaphors*

The allegorist acknowledges the visionary power of his linguistic medium. He sees through his language. Meta-phor, the vital principle of language, is also the animating force in allegory. It is because life can be seen as a journey, a quest, or a voyage that Dante, The Redcross Knight, or Gulliver can serve as examples of human behaviour, even though they exist for us in imaginary and non-realistic realms. John Barth has chosen two basic metaphors for his fabulative epic, which combine to make a dominant image from which many metaphorical consequences flow. He has chosen to see the universe as a university, and he has chosen to make his hero a man whose formative years were spent as a goat among goats. Before discussing the workings of the allegory itself, I want to consider the ap-propriateness of these two choices as metaphors for the human condition, and their effectiveness as basic materials for an allegorical narrative.

First, appropriateness. Language has provided the key to the first of these basic metaphors in the similarity of the words universe and university. The words are identical for three syllables, and then—worlds apart. But there is a meaningful connection between these two worlds. If the universe means *everything*—our whole world from the innermost piece of the smallest particle, outward to the ends of space, including those heavenly and hellish realms discerned only by poets and prophets—then the university means the place where *everything* is present as an object of inquiry and concern. For the thoughtful person, the world *is* a university, and his education always in process. For Barth, the university must have had the great virtue of including everything, already organized in terms of inquiry and quest. And beyond that, the American university of the present, though it strives to preserve an atmosphere of critical scrutiny and contemplation, is by no means an Arcadia studded with ivory towers where detached mandarins think beautiful thoughts. Despite its heritage from pagan academies and Christian cloisters, the modern American university is a brawling market place where CIA men mingle with student leftists, and careering business majors jostle with poets and painters. Not only is a university involved in the study and practice of politics in the statewide, national, and international spheres; it has its own internal politics, too. At some points, in fact, the two begin to merge. Men move back and forth between university posts and positions in government with increasing freedom. Concepts like the "multiversity" emphasize this particular penetration. And when the new governor of our most populous state, a man with Presidential aspirations, makes his first significant official act the firing of the head of that state's university system, who can say that the world is not in the university and the university in the world? It is precisely because the directors of universities, foundations, and corporations have become virtually interchangeable with high government officials—many of them serving Caesar and Socrates almost simultaneously—that Barth is able to get so much allegorical leverage from his selection of the university as his universe.

The appropriateness of his other fundamental metaphor should be equally evident. Again, language has provided the key. The connection between man and goat begins with the metaphorical application of the word for young goat to the young human. We all begin as kids. But if any particular kid should grow up to become a religious leader, the bringer of a new dispensation, a saviour who can expect ultimately that martyrdom with which mankind habitually reward their saints—then a whole new range of metaphorical materials comes into play; for we touch here on the connection between pastoral imagery and the religious life. This is the connection Milton exploited so powerfully in "Lycidas" by taking advantage of all the metaphorical implications of the word *pastoral*. Barth proceeds similarly. From goat-boy to scapegoat, the pilgrimage of George Giles ranges over the same metaphorical ground, only in comic and satyric fashion. From the traditional description of Christian judgment as a matter of separating "the sheep from the goats" Barth draws metaphoric strength. By making his "hero" a "goat" (an expression which in our idiom is paradoxical) he has chosen to upset the traditional Christian view of salvation. In tradition Christ, the Lamb of God, drove the pagan gods out of Europe and stilled forever the voice of the goatish Pan. Barth's *Revised New Syllabus* comically but seriously reinstates the goatish side of man. George is, as Stoker jokingly remarks, "Enos Enoch with balls"—a saviour who will restore sexuality to an honored place in human existence. In this respect

pasture; I romped without a care. In the fourteenth I slipped their gate—as I have since many another—looked over my shoulder, and saw that what I'd said bye-bye to was my happiness. (pp. 8–9)

It should be obvious that neither Barth nor his spokesman George is offering a recipe for the good life here; the speaker is commemorating his passage from kid-ship to man-hood, his departure from the world of animal happiness for the troubled world of men. This typical, this archetypal, journey is simply rescued by Barth from the realm of matter-of-course and given new life by his literalizing of the metaphor of child as kid and the consequent dramatization of the choice between animal simplicity and human complication. But to explore Barth's vision in any way approaching thoroughness we must move beyond these basic metaphors to their operation in the whole allegorical structure of the book.

B. *Allegorical Dimensions*

Allegory is notoriously an affair of "levels," but I should like to discard that notion—which implies more of a fixed hierarchy among kinds of meaning and a stricter separation among them than I believe exists, even in the great traditional allegories. Yet there are different meanings and different kinds of meaning in any richly imagined allegory. To encompass this variety of meaning without the unwelcome implications of "levels," I should like to consider the varieties of meaning in *Giles Goat-Boy* as facets or dimensions which become discernible to us when we consider the narrative from different angles of vision. This fabulation has, for example, its element of pure story or pure romance, the meanings of which are visceral rather than intellectual. These romance elements, however, are intimately connected with Barth's deliberate employment of myths and archetypes—dimensions of narrative that modern criticism is equipped to measure and understand. At the same time, the central events in the story of the hero's progress involve his adaptation of certain distinct ethical attitudes and his action according to those attitudes. The consequences of George's acting according to these different ethical attitudes lead him (and us) to evaluations of them, giving the book a philosophical dimension which is structurally central to the narrative. There are also important facets of *Giles Goat-Boy* that we might call sociological, psychological, and historical. We are used to thinking of matters of these latter kinds as the domain of realistic fiction rather than as allegorical facets of a work which is not essentially a piece of realism. This may make it hard for us to accept the validity of this dimension in a work of fabulation. Yet this is just what we must do in order to come to terms with Barth's narrative. Or, rather, it is one of a number of things we must do to grasp the whole narrative with full awareness of all its dimensions. For our reading of multi-dimensional allegory depends not only on our apprehending all the dimensions of the narrative, but also, even mainly, on our being aware of the interaction among them. In treating this sort of work, the critic must huff and puff along in an attempt to deal separately and statically with materials that function as a complex dynamic process in the work. Accordingly, I shall consider the allegory of *Giles Goat-Boy* under three main headings which reflect the three principal facets of the work. These rubrics (inevitably) are analogous to the main geographical divisions sketched out in the little fable that began the previous chapter: history (including social science), fiction (including myth), and philosophy (including theology).

C. History

I mean the term "history" in this sense to include every aspect of *Giles Goat-Boy* which points directly to the visible world as we know it. It will include, then, specific facts and individuals referred to—as Enos Enoch in *Giles* refers to Jesus Christ—and will also include the more general aspects of life as they are rendered intelligible for us by psychology and sociology. In terms of the book's historical frame of reference we can distinguish between a simple sort of allusion to a specific person or event under another name—as in the case of Enos Enoch—and a more complicated sort of allegorical allusion, through which a character or event in *Giles* acquires a discernible reference to a corresponding person or event in actuality without becoming entirely governed by or explainable in terms of that actuality. Max Spielman, for example, has overtones of Einstein and Oppenheimer specifically, but points more dimly to other figures, mainly Jewish, who have shaped modern life: Freud and Jung certainly, Marx possibly. Spielman also operates in a more general frame of reference, where he figures as a stereotypical Jew, and as the kind of scientist who retains his full humanity—compared to Eierkopf, whose narrow scientism is inhuman. Spielman, of course, is not merely historical in his allegorical dimensions. Seen in terms of myth, he is George's Mentor, the Chiron who sees to his education in a secluded retreat, the Vergil who guides him as far as reason can. In Eierkopf, on the other hand, the general references—positivistic

scientist—seem to outweigh any specific historical reference, and the ethical implications of his views are more
evident than any mythic implications derived from his
role in the narrative. Peter Greene and Leonid Andreich,
also, are far too complex to refer to any single individual.
Lucky Rexford, however, alludes strongly to John F. Kennedy in the specific frame of reference, but just as strongly
represents a type: the type of the good administrator, by
which Rexford is connected to fictional figures like Mel-
ville's Captain Vere or historical personages like Pontius
Pilate. Rexford and George are set to re-enact the archetypal confrontation between Pilate and prophet when *Giles
Goat-Boy* comes to an end.

This dimension of historical allusions also includes such
non-personal aspects as the way New Tammany refers to
the United States, Nikolay to Russia, and so on. This aspect of the allegory is actually quite superficial. It functions
merely to remind us that this is *not* a literal transcript of
Reality, and to cause us to re-see the countries referred
to in the new perspective provided by the allegory. All of
these specific references—the national and the personal
—have received some attention from the book's first reviewers. In fact, for many of them, these constituted the
entire allegorical aspect of the narrative. This is unfortunate, because this dimension is actually the least amusing
and the least significant in the whole fabulation, taken
by itself. Its main importance is that it leads toward the
other dimensions. It is essential that we take Lucky Rexford, for example, beyond the Kennedy reference to the
larger historical and mythic references his character and
actions generate. While it is true that Rexford's equivocal
brother, Stoker, can be seen as a Kennedy brother doing

the necessary dirty work behind the scenes to keep his sibling in power, Stoker must also be seen as a force necessarily opposed to Rexford's, and vital to Rexford's definition of himself and to his functioning: a parallel to Bray's opposition to George Giles.

These opposed pairs lead to the book's philosophical dimension, where the question of the relationship and purpose of Good and Evil is a principal concern, along with the implications of this relationship in the sphere of practical ethics. Rexford and Stoker, like Eierkopf and Croaker, or George and Bray, become a variant on the oriental symbol for necessary opposition: the balanced curvilinear forms of Yang and Yin. This symbol in black and white is echoed by the pairs mentioned here, but is also specifically invoked by the narrator to describe the positions of George and Anastasia descending in the elevator to WESCAC's belly. The struggle and necessary opposition of sexual embrace, thus finally embodies this same law of necessary opposition which is the guiding principle of the university as George learns to see it. Creation involves the kind of necessary and fruitful conflict symbolized by Yang and Yin and manifested in the sexual embrace. That is why proctoscopy repeats hagiography, why the freshman on his first *mons Veneris* and God creating the universe are archetypally related; and why, in fact, ontogeny recapitulates cosmogeny. The dimension of historical allusion, rightly understood, leads inevitably to the dimensions of philosophy and myth.

Some other characters will also serve to illustrate this principal of inter-connectedness among the allegorical dimensions of this tale. I am not sure whether Dr. Sear has any specific reference or not. But his name, suggesting a

brownish-yellow color (see his description on p. 188) and
the sound of the name, taken with the more general references to contemporary life that he seems to incorporate,
suggest that he may be a composite caricature of Norman
O. Brown and Timothy Leary. That decadent Freudianism
which leads to the cult of sensation and an infantile revelling in polymorphous perversity is frequently combined on
our campuses with a solemnly ritualized indulgence in
hallucinogens. Dr. Sear certainly points to the indulgence
of the senses, whether or not he refers as well to the high
priests usually invoked by the masters of such revelling.
And Sear's wasting disease, along with the change in his
attitude generated by the events of the narrative, point
just as clearly to Barth's condemnation of these forms of
self-indulgence.

Anastasia the heroine, like George the hero, alludes to
no particular person. Her Russian-sounding name reminds
us of Dostoevsky's Sonya, that prototype of the generous-
minded whore. But Barth locates Anastasia's generosity inside her sexual psychology rather than separate from it.
She is generous with herself because she is a masochist,
because she is a frigid, nymphomaniacal type—if we regard
her from the angle of clinical psychology. Yet she loves,
and this provides a different perspective on the same activities. Which is the true view? Leonid Andreich, Dostoevsky's countryman, sees her as a generous spirit. Peter
Greene, sentimental in a more Anglo-Saxon way, must
separate her into two women—the chaste Stacey and the
promiscuous Lacey. Dr. Sear regards her as an object or
instrument. For George, who is obliged to see through her,
she becomes the *other* person, who in the intimacy of sexual embrace helps to complete and define him. And he

urges her return to Stoker for the same reason. He needs her, she him. Anastasia also figures in the mythic dimension of the tale as a Beatrice figure, providing the revelation which completes George's education in humanity. But this revelation has not been spiritualized, as in the *Commedia*; it is a matter of the flesh. This is not, I should emphasize, a mere parody or burlesque of Dante, any more than D. H. Lawrence's *The Man Who Died* is just a joke on Jesus. Lawrence and Barth reject equally the medieval notion of an ideal future life: What is the best man can achieve in the flesh?, they ask.

The sociological dimension of the narrative functions in ways similar to the historical and psychological. The university metaphor operates here more restrictively perhaps than in other areas, for the life presented frequently takes its outward forms from college mores. The various student protesters, the lovemaking of the Be-ist in the buckwheat and his Chickie, the considerations of teaching methods and their computerization, as well as the treatment of academic minds in the persons of librarians and philosophers—all these are somewhat narrowly focused; but even here, in the few pointedly academic passages in the book, some extra-curricular things are going on. Consider this excerpt from Harold Bray's orientation lecture:

"For those with eyes to see New Tammany abounds with voiceless admonitions to humility. Not for nothing are 'Staff' and 'Faculty' equally privileged, so that groundskeepers and dormitory-cooks are affluent as new professors; not for nothing does custom decree that our trustees be unlettered folk, and that our chancellor be selected not from the intelligentsia but by ballot, from the lower percentiles: tinkers and tillers and keepers of shops. For the same reason one observes among the faculty not graybeard scholars only, their cowls ablazon with exotic marks of honor, but men of the people: former

*business majors, public-relations clerks, gentle carpenters and hus-
bandmen. It is fit that our libraries be more modest than our cow-
barns, our cow-barns than our skating-rinks, our skating-rinks than
our stadiums. Was not Enos Enoch, the Founder's Boy, by nature
an outdoor type, a do-it-Himselfer who chose as his original Tutees
the first dozen people He met; Who never took degree or published monograph or stood behind lectern, but gathered about Him
whoever would listen, in the buckwheat valleys or the wild rho-
dodendron of the slope, and taught them by simple fictions and
maxims proof against time, which are now graved in the limestone
friezes of our halls?"* (pp. 403–4)

Harold Bray is being serious and straightforward here.
And the state of affairs he depicts is a recognizable view of
the land-grant university as we encounter it in the United
States today. But the voice, as we listen to it, becomes
more and more familiar, the final description of Enos
Enoch reminding us of Bruce Barton's portrait of Jesus
as a businessman. This is the rhetoric of hucksterism, designed by Barth to be ironically seen through. Earlier, Bray
(the voice and name go together) has insisted, pragmati-
cally, that the undergraduate's only task is to *"Get the
Answers, by any means at all,"* adding that there is no
such thing as cheating, because *"To cheat can only mean
to Pass in ignorance of the Answers, which is impossible."*
Bray's emphasis on ends rather than means leads to a view
of the educational process in terms of the acquisition of a
degree rather than in terms of giving shape to a life. It is
oriented to appearances only, and salvation is not in it.
The clever peroration of the same speech, a prayer which
shrewdly talks down to the audience by merging the religious and the collegiate perspectives, is tainted with the
same "practical" ideology. The conflict between Bray and
George, which has its mythic and philosophical dimensions,
here takes its shape in terms of educational policy, as

George listens helplessly, dazzled by Bray's rhetorical display. The professor's prayer, as Bray formulates it, is firmly grounded in the sociology of the academy, from backseat to podium. But its fundamental attitude is at odds with George's, and its notion of salvation is opposed to the one George learns to value. Consider the clever close of the prayer:

". . . Be keg and tap behind the bar of every order, that the brothers may chug-a-lug Thy lore, see Truth in the bottom of their steins, and find their heads a-crack with insight. Be with each co-ed at the evening's close: paw her with facts, make vain her protests against learning's advances; take her to Thy mind's backseat, strip off preconceptions, let down illusions, unharness her from error—that she may ere the curfew be infused with Knowledge. Above all, Sir, stand by me at my lectern; be chalk and notes to me; silence the mowers and stay the traffic that I may speak; awaken the drowsy, confound the heckler; bring him to naught who would digress when I would not, and would not when I would; take my words from his mouth who would take them from mine; save me from slip of tongue and lapse of memory, from twice-told joke and unzippered fly. Doctor of doctors, vouchsafe unto me examples of the Unexampled, words to speak the Wordless; be now and ever my visual aid, that upon the empty slate of these young minds I may inscribe, bold and squeaklessly, the Answers!" (pp. 408–9)

This is, in a way, every professor's prayer, but it also exposes the absurdity of the professorial position, especially the position of the lecturer who seeks not to stimulate thought but to inculcate lessons—to brainwash. The infusion of knowledge can be seen as a backseat operation, only because one thinks of knowledge as a thing to be infused. Bray is successful in the academic sphere, much more so than George, because he gives the students what they want. But answers dispensed in such a way never turn out to be The Answers; these can never be given, only found. Bray's backseat image must be contrasted with George and Anastasia's lovemaking. In the difference between the furtive pleasure of a petting party gone the limit and the full and fertile union of two committed lovers, can be seen the difference between Bray's answers and those George finds with so much difficulty.

As he listens to Bray's speech, George himself is not experienced enough to see quite through it. But he learns from it that such an educational process is not for him: "Matriculation yes, class-attendance no; I must wrest my answers like swede-roots by main strength from their holes." Later, after experience has educated him, he sees the whole problem of Answers differently. In his final years, when twice interviewed by the journalism-majors, he has replied,

yes, I was the Grand Tutor, for better or worse, there was no help for it; yes, I knew what studentdom was pleased to call "The Answer" though that term—indeed the whole proposition—was as misleading as any other (and thus as satisfactory), since what I "knew" neither "I" nor anyone else could "teach," not even to my own Tutees. (p. 703)

Thus the sociology of the academy is connected by metaphoric strands to the philosophical dimension of the book through the notion of man's search for answers. By seeing the search too academically, Bray trivializes it. By seeing the limitations of any instructional apparatus, and beyond them the conceptual limitations of the whole notion of Answers, George reminds us of the feebleness of academic guideposts in a mysterious cosmos. The pedagogue on his podium is somewhere between Founder and freshman, related to both.

The whole range of social and historical data in *Giles*

Goat-Boy is impossible to trace without glossing virtually every page. Barth's employment of psychological perspectives similarly ranges from direct attention to the debauched Freudianism of Dr. Sear to the Jungian notion of archetypes which animates the cyclological theory of Max Spielman and the mythic structure of the story itself. And beyond this there is the vague but crucial dimension of psychological "rightness" in the responses of characters to situations. One might expect Anastasia, a creature fabricated from odds and ends of myth and psychoanalysis, to move as woodenly as Dr. Frankenstein's crude monster. But from her first siren-like appearance in the gorge to our last glimpse of her as the hard-eyed, nagging promoter of her kind of Gilesianism (keeping George at work on the Syllabus he does not want to record) she moves with a convincingness that is a tribute to Barth's perception of the way men and women actually behave. Effective allegory is never *merely* allegorical in its presentation of character and action.

Barth's insistence on "using stock figures, stereotype Jews and Negroes, just for fun" (as he said of *The Sot-Weed Factor*) is carried even further in *Giles Goat-Boy*. Spielman talks an absurd stage-Yiddish kind of English, for example, and the Peter Greene-Leonid Andreich duo are distinguished by equally blatant tricks of speech. These thick crusts of type-characterization certainly obliterate any potential for profoundly developed individual personalities. Such characters are closer to pre-novelistic kinds of characterization than to the deep individuality of the realists. Their vitality is mainly a matter of accumulated facets and functions rather than an accretion of telling idiosyncracies. Yet Barth has learned enough from the realists—as his first two novels show—to make stereotypes like Greene and Spielman behave with psychological rightness, even when their behavior is heavily burdened with mythic or ethical implications. The loss of each of Greene's eyes, for example, is a bizarre and improbable event, important in its ethical implications, comic and pathetic in its immediate narration, and presented with an emotional appropriateness that justifies the improbability of the actual event and the weight of allegory that it supports. Greene's innocent narration of the loss of his first eye (pp. 233–5) is too long to quote and too fine to summarize, but I offer it as evidence of the astonishing way Barth can move his narrative along, invent bizarrely symbolic events, and generate in the reader amusement, pity, sympathy, derision, and all manner of high and low thoughts—carrying conviction on all levels from the immediate to the remotest reaches of the allegory. Greene's whole narrative, the archetypal history of the American WASP, complete with triumphs and the neuroses appropriate to them, failures and the faults responsible for them, is a masterful job in the dimension of history, sociology, and psychology. It is probably Barth's strongest performance in this dimension in *Giles Goat-Boy*. I urge the reader to see it for himself.

D. Philosophy

This fabulation has other aspects which must be explored, even at the expense of leaving much unsaid about its historical dimension. The story of George the Goat-Boy, which is at the heart of the narrative, itself points in two major directions: outward toward the mythic area which correlates all experience in terms of great archetypal patterns, and inward toward a single philosophical position which may be regarded as the moral of this great fabulation. (If I have understood rightly the meaning of Henry James's esthetic parable "The Figure in the Carpet," James sees the literary artist and the critic as totally separate in their functions. The writer must have his entire say about the meaning of his work through the work itself. Those words once said, he must remain mute and rely on his audience to understand. The critic functions simply as the spearhead of that audience. It is his job, above all, to understand, to see the figure in the carpet and perhaps even to expound it —a thing he can do and the author cannot, precisely because his words have no claim to authority beyond their more or less convincing exposition of the text. I accept James's view—as I understand it—and will try to present here an interpretation of the central figure in Barth's great Arabian rug.)

Such aspects of this figure as belong mainly to myth, I set aside for the moment, to touch on them later. The philosophical dimension of the narrative is my concern here. And in dealing with it I must confess that I am not a philosopher. I cannot go quite so far as Barth himself, who says "I don't know anything about philosophy. I've never even studied it, much less learned it." But I do have only the slenderest experience of formal philosophical discipline. Barth's own disclaimer, I am inclined to take with some grains of salt. He is certainly an amateur of philosophy, and a professional at dealing with philosophical materials in narrative form (an art that few professional philosophers master—see Iris Murdoch's criticisms of Sartre in her *Sartre, Romantic Rationalist*, for example).

The moral of this fabulation emerges from the events of

George's life, and in particular from his dialectical progress in trying to work out a Grand Tutorial philosophy. I call this process dialectical because its three main phases—thesis, antithesis, and synthesis—are unmistakable. They are correlated in the narrative with George's three descents to WESCAC's belly, and all the actions and advice associated with those three descents.

George's first Grand Tutorial posture, which I call Thesis, is formulated on page 420 and repeated in the form of advice up through his first descent (p. 507 ff.). This view —"that the first reality of life on campus must be the clear distinction between Passage and Failure"—leads George to a posture of fundamentalist righteousness. The advice which follows from it, in every sphere from personal relations to the boundary dispute between the East and West Campuses, is disastrous. This Thesis, in fact, is so intolerable that we shall do well to look into the way it is fashioned. George first formulates it in a dispute with Stoker ("more in hopes of unsettling my adversary than of instructing either him or myself"). It is a debating point originally, a mere piece of rhetoric, but, as so often happens in life and in fiction, George becomes a prisoner of his rhetoric and finally begins to believe it; even though in this early phase of his acceptance of the Thesis he feels that there is "some murky valid *point* in Stoker's life, which I could not as yet assimilate." It is no wonder that when he emerges from WESCAC's belly he wears the mask of Harold Bray. Like Bray, he has not Answers to offer, but empty rhetoric. But unlike Bray, he believes his own formulations. And the reader, wishing George well and wanting him to succeed in his quest, inevitably grants George's Thesis some degree of empathetic assent, thus entangling himself emotionally and intellectually in the dialectical process.

George's second Grand Tutorial posture is the Antithesis of the first. He arrives at this Antithesis while munching pages of the original New Syllabus—Enos Enoch's Testament. The passage illustrates so well the convincingness with which Barth renders such a bizarre episode—the rightness of the attitudes involved, the solidity of the detail —that I quote it at some length. The incident takes place in Main Detention, where George is temporarily imprisoned. In the excitement after Leonid has attempted suicide, George is left with his demented mother, who used to feed him in this manner when he was a kid:

Crosslegg`ed on the floor, black-shawled and -dressed, the New Syllabus on her lap as always, she flapped at me her thrice-weekly peanut-butter sandwich and crooned, "Come, Billy! Come, love! Come!"

Anxious as I was for my Nikolayan cellmate, I laid my head in her lap, pretended to hunger for the ritual food, and chewed the pages of antique wisdom she tore out for me, though they tasted sourly of much thumbing.

"Now then, love, let me see . . ." She adjusted her spectacles, brightly licked her forefingertip, and opened the book to a dogeared page. "People ought to use bookmarks!" she fussed. "And there's a verse marked, too. People *shouldn't* mark in library-books." Her tone softened. "Oh, but look what it is, Billikins: I'm *so* proud of the things you write!"

Such was her gentle madness, she thought me at once Billy Bocksfuss in the hemlock-grove, the baby GILES she'd bellied —and, alas, the long-Commenc`ed Enos Enoch.

"*Pass`ed are the flunked*," she read, very formally. "My, but that's a nice thought. Don't you think?"

I didn't answer, not alone because my tongue was peanut-buttered, but because those dark and famous words from the Seminar-on-the-Hill brought me upright. As lightning might a

man bewildered, they showed me in one flash the source and nature of my fall, the way to the Way, and, so I imagined, the far
gold flicker of Commencement Gate. (p. 551)

This moment of illumination leads George to formulate
his new view that "*failure is passage*." This new answer,
with its beguiling paradoxes, proves finally to be as rhetorical as the first, though the rhetoric this time is not that of
fundamentalist preaching but of semantic philosophizing.
The absurd wordiness associated with this posture is exposed not only by the horrible results of the new advice
founded on it (total anarchy, the dangerously insane set
"free," etc.) but directly in a passage in which George has
a one-way conversation with the Living Sakhyan, with
choral commentary from a group of student protesters.
This audience affects George much the same way that
Stoker did in the formulation of his original Thesis. He
shows off verbally for their appreciation. But the approval
of these lads is, in the full context, a criticism. Their readi-
ness to "go limp" is an outward sign of their spiritual flabbi-
ness. All too easily they can verbalize themselves into a
state of wordless apathy based on their knowledge of the
arbitrariness of categories. Since everything is arbitrary,
nothing matters. Limpness is all.

The final absurdity of the limp view of life is exposed in
George's second descent to WESCAC's belly. There, called
upon to designate his sex, he reasons thus: "what were
male and *female* if not the most invidious of the false
polarities into which undergraduate reason was wont to
sunder Truth." This denial of sex, already rendered absurd
by the floroscopic episode (quoted above, p. 139), is an
attempt to deny the principle of creation through division,
upon which all higher life is founded. These categories,

which George would abolish, are not merely WESCAC's, they are life's. In denying them, George denies the very dialectical process he is involved in, denies his separation from and attraction to Anastasia. If failure is passage, then death is life.

George persists in this fatal view until, with the University crumbling into chaos around him, he is confronted with the now completely blinded Peter and Leonid, hand-cuffed together in Stoker's sidecar. Stoker asks him, "So there they sit, Goat-Boy: two blind bats! Are they passed or failed?" This question drives George once again over the questions he has thought settled, fetching him "from apathy into the intensest concentration" of his life:

Indeed it was not I concentrating, but something concentrating upon me, taking me over, like the spasms of defecation or labor-pains. Leonid Andreich and Peter Greene—their estates were rather the occasion than the object of this concentration, whose real substance was the fundamental contradictions of failure and pas-sage. Truly now those paradoxes became paroxysms. . . . That circular device on my assignment sheet—beginningless, endless, infinite equivalence . . . constricted my reason like a torture tool from the Age of Faith. Passage *was* Failure, and Failure Passage; yet Passage was Passage, Failure Failure! Equally true, none was the Answer; the two were not different, neither were they the same; and *true* and *false*, and *same* and *different*— Unspeakable! Un-namable! Unimaginable! Surely my mind must crack! (pp. 649–50)

At this moment, as George strains to face and subdue the questions he has dodged around with rhetorical gimmicks, the tension mounts and Stoker shouts a warning to his prisoners:

"Don't try to get loose!" No doubt it was Leonid Stoker warned, but his words struck my heart, and I gave myself up utterly to that which bound, possessed, and bore me. I let go, I let all go; relief went through me like a purge. And as if in signal of my freedom, over the reaches of the campus the bells of Tower Clock suddenly rang out, somehow unjammed: their first full striking since the day I'd passed through Scrapegoat Grate. As I listened astonished, the strokes mounted—*one, two, three, four*—each bringing from my pressèd eyes the only tears they'd spilled since a fateful late-June morn many terms past, out in the barns. *Sol, la, ti,* each a tone higher than its predecessor, unbinding, releasing me—then *do:* my eyes were opened; I was delivered. (pp. 650–51)

The last note, musically the octave-completing *do,* stands also for the simple imperative urging action: do!

This is Synthesis. Passage and failure are distinct but interdependent. They define one another and are as necessary as North and South or male and female to the functioning of the universe. Action by each individual, appropriate to himself and his situation, discovered by the dialectic process of trial and error, is the only way to salvation. Thus there are no formulas. The *Revised New Syllabus* is not a catechism but the story of one man's heroic attempt to work out his own life and find his own truth. The philosophical dimension of this book emphasizes the isolation of the individual and the loneliness of his way. We are left finally without a moral. We are given only the story of a life to imitate, with the qualification that to imitate it we must diverge from it, since George's life is his; ours, ours. But because this life itself resembles other lives that we know through fiction and history, we know that we shall have companions in our loneliness. What philosophy sunders, myth unites, and philosophy is only one facet of this fabulation.

E. Fiction and Myth

The moral evaporates in our hands; the story remains with us. And since the moral urges the advantages of action over ratiocination, this is appropriate enough. Actually, the philosophical dimension of the narrative functions mainly as a story within the larger story of George's adventures. It is appropriately concerned with the academic side of George's experience—from matriculation to graduation. It is an intellectual episode in a sequence of more physical adventures to which it is connected in many ways—most importantly as the pivotal achievement which releases George from intellectual concerns so that he can complete his other tasks. In effect, by defining "himself," George prepares for true recognition of the "other" in Anastasia. Their union in WESCAC's belly is the physical ratification of George's intellectual achievement. This act of love, and the idyllic interlude at the farm which follows it, end the erotic romance plot of the narrative. This consummation in turn frees George for his final work. Having found himself and won the lady, he must slay the dragon. That is, he must drive Harold Bray off the face of the campus. Bray is his work, as necessary to his completion in the realm of action as Anastasia is to his personal completion.

In the world of this book there are no loose ends, because *its* creator is not a realist. The world we live in is another matter. Though we can learn from the world of George and Anastasia, we cannot enter that world. It is resolutely fictional—the world of the fabulator. Barth insists on the non-reality of his world in many ways, of which I wish to point out just one, before turning to a consideration of the way the mythic and philosophical dimensions of the narrative are interrelated. The episode I have in mind occurs on George's last trip to the Belfry. After refusing to answer the scholars' request for a gloss on the crucial *lacuna* in the Founder's Scroll (*"Flunkèd who would Pass or Passèd are the Flunked"*), George approaches a librarian to ask if there is a way up beside the guarded elevator:

The pimpled maid, thin and udderless as Mrs. Rexford but infinitely less prepossessing, looked over her spectacles from the large novel she was involved in and said with careful clarity—as if that question, from a fleecèd goat-boy at just that moment were exactly what she'd expected— "Yes. A stairway goes up to the Clockworks from this floor. You may enter it through the little door behind me."

All the while she marked with her finger her place in the book, to which she returned at once upon delivering her line. Mild, undistinguished creature, never seen before or since, whose homely face I forgot in two seconds; whose name, if she bore one, I never knew; whose history and fate, if any she had, must be *lacunae* till the end of terms in my life's story— Passage be yours, for that in your moment of my time you did announce, clearly as from a written text, your modest information. Simple answer to a simple question, but lacking which this tale were as truncate as the Founder's Scroll, an endless fragment!

"*-less fragment*," I thought I heard her murmur as I stooped through the little door she'd pointed out. I paused and frowned; but though her lips moved on, as did her finger across the page, her words were drowned now by the bells of Tower Clock. (p. 666)

This girl "delivers her line" so perfectly because she is reading it out of the book in front of her. In fact she is reading this particular book: *Giles Goat-Boy*. She is where she is; the staircase is where it is; everything in this tale is where it is because it was made that way by its fabricator. This "tale" would indeed be "truncate" if she and her staircase were not there. They are in place because Barth is a fabulator, and he is gently and wittily reminding us of that, reminding us that our world and this one are different, different. But at the same time he is working toward mythic connections through which we can perceive the dimensions of our own lives that transcend the individual and personal to partake of something universal.

The mythic dimension of *Giles Goat-Boy* has necessarily impinged on every aspect of my discussion in this chapter. Yet more remains to be done with it than I can do. It would be possible to trace through all the Oedipal allusions in the book, from the exuberant parody, *Taliped Decanus*, through the Freudian implications of the myth as they relate to George's own behavior or that of the other central characters, to its connection with the theme of blindness and vision in the tale. Such a glossing would reveal the astonishing interconnectedness of the narrative itself, and at the same time would illuminate one passage of connection between the mythic and the experiential worlds. Similarly, one could trace through the Dantesque, the Quixotic, the Ulyssean, the Mosaic allusions, showing how the human truth embodied in these myths is reinvigorated by the new combinations of them assembled in this chronicle of heroic action. All this, given world enough and time, one could do. But I believe the alert reader picks up many of these threads without assistance, some consciously and others subliminally, so that such glossing is not really necessary. And besides, to take the mythography of *Giles Goat-Boy* in too heavy a way would do the story violence. Barth's vision, like Joyce's, holds myth and comedy in a precarious balance. There are reasons beyond any question of affinity or influence why two such gifted writers treat mythic materials comically; and before returning for a last look at myth and philosophy in *Giles Goat-Boy*, I should like to consider these reasons, since they bear importantly on the whole matter of fabulation as a modern mode of fiction.

The mythic and archetypal dimension of literature,

fundamental as it is, has only recently begun to be understood. That is, a criticism and understanding of fiction based upon an awareness of the archetypal patterns of mythology and their relationship to the human psyche is a fairly recent development. As a result of this new understanding and the proliferation of literary studies based upon it, some influential critics have been ready to proclaim a new age of myth as the most likely literary development of the immediate future. But this, it seems to me, is the least likely of literary developments. Once so much is known *about* myths and archetypes, they can no longer be used innocently. Even their connection to the unconscious finally becomes attenuated as the mythic materials are used more consciously. All symbols become allegorical to the extent that we understand them. Thus the really perceptive writer is not merely conscious that he is using mythic materials: He is conscious that he is using them consciously. He *knows*, finally, that he is allegorizing. Such a writer, aware of the nature of categories, is not likely to believe that his own mythic lenses really capture the truth. Thus his use of myth will inevitably partake of the comic.

Every one of the fabulators I have considered can be called a comic writer, even John Hawkes, whose vision is the darkest. Fabulation, then, seems to partake inevitably of the comic. It derives, I would suggest, from the fabulator's awareness of the limits of fabulation. He knows too much—that is the modern writer's predicament, and that is precisely what prevents his perspective from being seriously mythic. This quotation from Barth's interview in *Wisconsin Studies* bears on the point I am trying to make:

Somebody told me I must have had in mind Lord Raglan's twenty-five prerequisites for ritual heroes when I created the character of Ebenezer Cooke in *The Sot-Weed Factor*. I hadn't read Raglan so I bought *The Hero*, and Ebenezer scored on twenty-three of the twenty-five, which is higher than anybody else except Oedipus. If I hadn't lied about Ebenezer's grave, I would have scored twenty-four. Nobody knows where the real chap is buried; I made up a grave for Ebenezer because I wanted to write his epitaph. Well, subsequently I got excited over Raglan and Joseph Campbell, who may be a crank for all I know or care, and I really haven't been able to get that business off my mind—the tradition of the wandering hero. The only way I could use it would be to make it comic, and there will be some of that in *Giles Goat-Boy*.

There is, of course, more than a little of "that" in *Giles Goat-Boy*. From George's mysterious birth to his anticipated disappearance, his life falls into Lord Raglan's pattern, which is to say into the great patterns of primitive myth and the major literary treatments of myth. And so, up to a point, do all our lives. Insofar as Spielman's Law is valid in the experiential world, all our lives have archetypal significance: Myth tells us that we are all part of a great story. But the fabulators, so clearly aware of the difference between fact and fiction, are unwilling to accept the mythic view of life as completely valid. Against this view they balance one which I am calling the philosophical, which tells us that every man is unique, alone, poised over chaos. In *Giles Goat-Boy*, for example, the great computer WESCAC functions mythically as the father-god engaged in the archetypal struggle with the son who seeks to displace him. But George's final view specifically repudiates this mythic perspective on his father:

I had been wrong, I said, to think it Troll. Black gap and gown of naked Truth, it screened from the general eye what only a few, Truth's lovers and tutees, might look on bare and not be blinded.

(p. 676)

Here the philosophical view dominates. But myth prevails in George's struggle with Bray, his proper adversary.

Throughout *Giles Goat-Boy* and throughout modern fabulation these two perspectives on experience engage like
Yang and Yin in equal struggle for control. This mighty
tension is at the heart of Barth's great fabulation and all
the rest. Just as the realistic novel was rooted in the conflict between the individual and society, fabulation springs
from the collision between the philosophical and mythic
perspectives on the meaning and value of existence, with
their opposed dogmas of struggle and acquiescence. If
existence *is* mythic, then man may accept his role with
equanimity. If not, then he must struggle through part
after part trying to create one uniquely his own. Barth
and the other fabulators build on the interinanimation of
these two views. All our assignment-sheets, they tell us, are
stamped like George's: Pass All/Fail All.

INDEX

Note: This is an index to authors and titles only. More general subjects are indicated by the chapter and sub-chapter headings given in the table of contents. Titles of works are listed under the author entry in so far as possible.

177

DATE DUE			
FEB 22 74			
MAY 7 1975			
DEC 14 84			
DEC 14 1981			